UNBREAKABLE

UNBREAKABLE

BREAKING THE SILENCE.
FINDING MY VOICE.
SHARING MY STORY.

BY CAROLYN SOPHIA SKOWRON

NEW DEGREE PRESS

UNBREAKABLE

Breaking the Silence. Finding my Voice. Sharing my Story.

ISBN   978-1-63676-960-8   *Paperback*

978-1-63730-026-8   *Kindle Ebook*

978-1-63730-128-9   *Ebook*

I dedicate this book to my fighter and unbreakable best friend, Ali.

Another person this is dedicated to is to my angel, Nomi.

Lastly, I dedicate this book to my incredible mom, dad, and sister.

Contents

PART 1

Introduction

———

Stigma: A mark of shame or discredit. [1]

Imperfections are not what break you—they are what make you.

My life has flashed before my eyes not once but twice. All through my teenage years, I was struggling silently with my mental health. I started to lose hope and never spoke a word of it. I felt isolated, broken, and beyond worthless. Saying "I'm fine" was my go-to because I did not want to admit I was in a dark place. I was silently struggling with depression, anxiety, and as much as it pains me to say, self-harm. I refused to admit I had serious mental health issues that needed to be addressed and thought I was "fine." I would not talk about how I was feeling, so I built up this exterior to hide my emotions. I refused to open up. I mean REFUSED. I kept everything to myself, which eventually backfired once I got to college.

———

1   *Merriam-Webster, s.v.* "stigma (n.)," accessed December 19, 2020.

My freshman year was the worst year of my life. Every day was a struggle. Each day I kept feeling more and more depressed. One fall night I heard people laughing and talking with their friends as I was sitting on my bed in my dorm room all alone. I wondered why everyone else seemed so happy; I had nothing to live for and had hit rock bottom. I questioned who I was and if I was worth anything because I did not have friends to go with to the dining hall, let alone friends in general. I would not leave my dorm room and that particular night, my depression got so bad I wanted to end it all. All I could think about was ending my pain. I just wanted to be done with life and I thought suicide would be the answer to my problem. **It was not.**

My story could have ended way too soon, before I could grow into who and what I wanted to become; however, thanks to my faith, my best friends, and my family, I have learned that embracing my flaws is the key to living a valuable and purposeful life. Imperfections are what make life so beautiful. Nothing is or ever will be perfect. We all have a different story and different battles with which we are dealing.

Even celebrities have struggles because no matter who we are, we are human. A particular inspiration to me is Selena Gomez. She cares for people and wants to help others because she is *real*. She is open about her struggles with mental health issues and vulnerable with the entire world. No one really knew about her struggle with depression and anxiety (and this year diagnosed with bipolar disorder) until the 2016 American Music Awards. When she won "Favorite Pop/Rock Female Artist," Selena gave an incredibly powerful speech.

In 2014, this stage was actually the first time that I was authentically 100 percent honest with all of you. I think it's safe to say that most of you know a lot of my life, whether I liked it or not. And I had to stop. Because I had everything, and I was absolutely broken inside. And I kept it all together enough to where I would never let you down, but I kept it too much together to where I let myself down. [2]

This quote is so powerful because it shows that **no one** has their life all together, no matter who you are. We just do not—but we try. While I was growing up, I was so insecure with myself that I never felt I could be real and authentic with anyone. I had no idea where I fit in or where I belonged. The older I got, the more insecure I became. I **never** felt good enough, and for the longest time, I struggled in silence. I could not express what was really going on. There was a dark cloud constantly looming over my head. I was numb to the world and faked my way through each day.

What is the biggest reason I kept everything to myself?

Stigma.

I always felt I needed to please everyone else. My feelings didn't matter, so I never used my voice. I hid my feelings because I wanted to fit into society. Even when I was asked what was wrong, I refused to say anything. I did not want to tell my family and friends how hopeless I felt since it was not a problem they could solve. Hell, it was not a problem I

---

2   Alyssa Bailey, "I Had Everything, but I Was Broken Inside," *ELLE*, October 11, 2017.

could solve. Not yet. My silence and isolation grew to feelings of destruction and despair.

Keeping my mental health issues a secret was easier in the short term, but definitely more detrimental to my mental health in the long term. It took me a while to open up to my family because I did not want them to worry. I had everything I could ever ask for: I went to an amazing school, I had my own car, and never wanted for anything. I am beyond thankful and blessed for the upbringing I had and the amazing resources I was given, but at the same time, I felt this constant pressure to hide what was going on with me to protect my "image." There were times I was ashamed and guilty. In my head, there was this stereotype: I was not allowed to feel sad or be upset because I was "privileged," and people had bigger problems than I did. Regardless, I know now my feelings were still real.

Self-doubt and self-deprecation were things I suffered far too often. I was shy because it was the only way to not say the wrong thing. In a TED Talk given by Jennifer Cohen, she expressed how important it was to sometimes take a risk and fail, rather than never try at all. There was one particular moment where she talked about being "out there," something I was too scared to do because being "out there" and "bold" terrified me.

"Boldness is a stronger indicator of success than intelligence is. This is because smart people think of all the negative things that can happen when things go wrong, but bold people think of all the good things that will happen when things go right." [3]

3   Jennifer Cohen, "The Secret to Getting Anything You Want in Life," filmed October 20, 2019, at TEDxBuckhead, Atlanta, GA, *YouTube*, Video, 16:01.

Living with this mindset, I became much more fulfilled with my life because it helped me find happiness within myself. This only happened after I stopped pretending to be everything I was not and focused on everything I was. My sister helped turn my life around. She asked me,

*"What life **do you want** for yourself?"*

This hit me hard. When I thought about what I wanted, it was to be happy. I needed to accept that she was right, get out of my own way, and get help. Going to therapy is when my relationship with myself changed for the better. I found the real me and became the best version of myself. It was a process which took a great deal of time and different therapists. Truly, in the beginning, I did not think it was possible to be happy. If you have ever thought the same, trust me, I get it, but it *is* possible. I know hearing "you need help" sucks, but it can also be the best words you will ever hear. Help is what saved me. If you are ever ashamed about seeking help, similar to how I was, don't be. We are all people. We all have problems.

Mental illnesses are common in the United States. Nearly one in five U.S. adults live with a mental illness (51.5 million in 2019). Mental illnesses include many different conditions that vary in degree of severity, ranging from mild to moderate to severe. Two broad categories can be used to describe these conditions: Any Mental Illness (AMI) and Serious Mental Illness (SMI). AMI encompasses all recognized mental illnesses. SMI is a smaller and more severe subset of AMI. [4]

---

4   National Institute of Mental Health, "Mental Illness," last updated January 2021, accessed January 31, 2021.

Truthfully, we live in a toxic world. We try constantly to measure up to some preconceived notion of perfection by comparing ourselves to each other. We are losing more and more people each day because we say hurtful words and are hateful and judgmental instead of being loving and understanding. We do not need to compare. We need to care for each other. Respect is something we all deserve. Why do we fail to do this so often? You cannot control what the person next to you is doing, but you can control what you do.

Social media should be fun. There is no reason we need to make our lives look perfect. We edit our pictures and only post the good ones. That is not real life. What if we could help the suicide rate go down? How amazing would that be?

Let's start by trying to build each other up. We can be the ones to better the lives of future generations if we start now with something as small as:

- Show a simple act of kindness
- Smile at others
- Reach out to an old friend
- Send a friendly text

Many ways exist to help pull a person out of darkness. I have written this book to show some of my struggles, including those my generation deals with every day. I hope as I share my story that it will help you be more vulnerable and heal in your own way. After you read this, I want you to be able to live your best life simply by being the best you—the real you. Whether you struggle with your own mental health or love someone who does, know there is a light at the end of the tunnel. There is help. There is recovery. There is hope.

Embrace the fact that we are all perfectly imperfect!

CHAPTER 1

Darkness of Bullying

Bullying: Abuse and mistreatment of someone vulnerable by someone stronger, more powerful, etc.; the actions and behavior of a bully. [5]

Have you ever felt like you were not enough no matter what you did? We often get in our heads that we are not enough. Not attractive enough, not skinny enough, we don't have enough friends. Just not enough. **Enough** *to being not enough!*

Feeling as though I was not enough started at a young age. When I was a kid in elementary school, I let the "not enough" thought get into my head. This started when I was in third grade. Yes, you read that right. In third grade I already felt I was not enough and did not belong. This was where the downward spiral to my life began and only continued to get worse as I got older. I would do anything and everything to fit in. I would change myself in order for people to like me. I never let myself just be me.

---

5   *Merriam-Webster*, s.v. "bullying (*n.*)," accessed August 27, 2020.

You are enough *means that you don't have to strive to become more worthy, more valid, more acceptable, or more loved. You already are all of those things. There are things you might want to be more of. More open. More honest. More true. More authentic. More free. More connected. More intentional. More purposeful. Those are all expressions of your enough-ness. They aren't about changing yourself, they're about being yourself...You were enough before, you are enough now, and you will continue to be enough as you become more of who you were made to be.* And believing that, when the world keeps whispering otherwise, is brave. [6]

My childhood would not exactly be defined as a glorious time socially. I was usually being pushed around. I was bullied and never fit in. I did not have the courage to say no to people, and because of that, I was used and taken advantage of. I never stood my ground because I was too scared of what others would think. Since I got shut down, speaking up and talking were never something I did. I was timid and shy.

Finding my voice and who I was did not happen until many years later. I did not feel enough for friends. I did not feel enough for guys. I never felt I was enough for anyone. Everyone wanted something better, and I was not it. I did not see myself as enough. From a young age I did not fit in, and I knew it. Eight-year-old Carolyn really set the tone of how I would take compliments and rejection later in life. As a child, I couldn't have imagined that my confidence would be

---

6   Melissa Camara Wilkins, "What It Means to Be Enough," (blog), accessed January 4, 2021.

nonexistent at such a young age. Some people might think elementary school would not be too bad, let alone third grade, because all you really do is learn the multiplication table. That was not my reality. Reality for me was an absolute nightmare. I felt alone. When someone is not nice to you, it can hurt your feelings; when someone wants you dead, that's another story.

One day, I walked into my classroom after recess and saw a piece of paper that said, "Kill Carolyn."

Immediately, my heart started racing and I felt this horrible pain in my stomach. I was just a little eight-year-old girl who wanted to play with her Polly Pockets in peace and not worry about anything else. Instead, I got the feeling that I sucked, and no one liked me. I did not belong, like an outcast. I had no friends to have play dates with after school and no matter what I did, I felt worthless. I thought the rest of the kids did not like me and because of that, I started to not like myself. I questioned what I was doing wrong, but I could never figure out what that was.

Seeing that note made me vulnerable and scared. I ran to the bathroom and bawled my eyes out. How could someone be so cruel? How could another eight-year-old be so vicious with their words and actions? I was confused and did not know what I did wrong. I came to a skewed perception that it was a "me" thing. I truly thought as a kid, *maybe there is something wrong with me and maybe I am the problem.* I started to almost hyperventilate, and I did not know what to do. I was sad and unworthy, but the reality was, *I did nothing wrong.* Being a kid and being hard on yourself can be one thing, but it became my whole thought process. Anxiety started to become part of me. How was I supposed to know about anxiety at eight years old?

The American Academy of Child and Adolescent Psychiatry states that a death threat is not something to be taken lightly.

When a child makes a serious threat, it should not be dismissed as just idle talk. Parents, teachers, or other adults should immediately talk with the child. If it is determined that the child is at risk and/or the child refuses to talk, is argumentative, responds defensively, or continues to express violent or dangerous thoughts or plans, arrangements should be made for an **immediate assessment** *by a mental health professional with experience evaluating children and adolescents.* [7]

This trauma was an event that affected me deeply and didn't surface until many years later.

Traumatic stressors such as early trauma can lead to post-traumatic stress disorder (PTSD), which affects about 8% of Americans at some time in their lives, as well as depression, substance abuse, dissociation, personality disorders, and health problems. For many trauma victims, PTSD can be a lifelong problem. [8]

---

7   *American Academy of Child and Adolescent Psychiatry,* "Threats by Children: When Are they Serious?" American Academy of Child & Adolescent Psychiatry, no. 65 (January 2019): accessed September 21, 2020.

8   J. Douglas Bremner, "Traumatic Stress: Effects on the Brain," *Dialogues in Clinical Neuroscience 8, no.4,* (December 2006).

Any trauma experienced as a kid sits far in front of your brain. Knowing this now, it was not my fault I had a hard time focusing in class.

Third Grade, Take Two

Fast forward a year and I went to a new school. It was safe to say the bullying at my old school affected me academically to the point that I did not get much out of that previous year. Because of this, I had to repeat third grade. Going to a new school did not make me feel I was getting a fresh start because I was held back. I felt stupid. Being so young and told you are going to need to repeat the same thing *again* is quite a scary thing to hear. This immediately made me feel different and dumber than everyone else. If anyone ever asked me why I was so "old" for my grade, I told them I went to preschool late, so I was not looked down upon.

Looking back, I now see that repeating a grade or taking longer than your peers is not a big deal. Actually, it can set you up for more success. I did not need to compare myself to what those around me were doing. It was what I needed to do for me. Research shows that my experience is shared.

New research from Harvard Graduate School of Education professor Martin West tells a nuanced and evidence-based story about grade retention, finding that—contrary to crit-ics' fears—repeating third grade does not reduce students' chances of completing high school. In fact, it improves their preparedness for high school and their performance while enrolled...Roughly 10 percent of children in the United States are retained at least once between kindergarten and eighth grade, West writes. Those rates could rise in the coming years, since sixteen states and the District of Columbia have enacted policies requiring that students who do not demonstrate basic reading proficiency when they first take state tests in third grade be held back. Florida has been the model for states adopting these policies; in 2002, it mandated that low-scoring third graders be retained and receive remedial services. [9]

Middle School

In middle school, I was scared to attend. Anxiety starting to build up and I would do anything I could to be "sick." Clearly there was an issue, but what really set me off was an afternoon after recess (this seems to be a theme). I came back to my desk when I noticed a paper on the table behind me with a drawing and some writing. It read, "Marvin the Martian."

The Marvin picture was me. It was a drawing of me with frizzy hair, yellow teeth, and a huge nose. The nose was drawn completely out of scale and drawn much bigger than it actually was, but I felt humiliated. I became even more insecure about my appearance. It made me hate my nose and after that I did not want to show my face in school ever again. I was upset and sad. My anxiety and the feeling of not being enough continued into my whole thought process of how I thought of myself for the longest time.

---

9   Casey Bayer, "When Kids Are Held Back, Gains Can Follow," *Usable Knowledge*, Harvard Graduate School of Education, July 2017, accessed September 21, 2020.

Bullying makes you feel something is wrong with you and that you do not belong, even though it is **not** your fault.

Lessons Learned

1. *I Was Not Alone*

I was surprised at how many famous people have gone through bullying as well. Blake Lively, one of my favorite actresses, is a good influence. She put a positive spin on the bullying that happened to her at a young age. She posted a photo of her with Sesame Street's Big Bird on social media saying: "Kids used to make fun of me in elementary school by calling me Big Bird (because I was too tall and had yellow hair). Here's to making best buddies with the things that once hurt you." [10]

2. *Humor Helps*

The way Lively was able to put an encouraging spin on something that once affected her deeply is a great way to deal with hate and negativity. It was not until many years later that I was able to laugh at the Marvin jokes and make light of them. Adversity makes you stronger because it can make you more resilient. For me, confidence took years to build. The biggest thing that helped me is to not take life so seriously. I can be a bit klutzier than most people, but I can now laugh at myself and make a joke of it.

---

10   Maria Yagoda, "Shawn Mendes, Lady Gaga, & More Stars Who've Opened up about the Bullying They Faced as Kids," *People*, November 20, 2019.

3. Understand Why Children Bully

An article from *The Huffington Post* states:

The trait that all bullies have in common is insecurity.[11]

Bullies who said and did horrible things must have been so insecure with themselves. Instead of dealing with their emotions, they turned to bullying me to cover up their insecurity. This was a way for them to not think about their own problems. When I thought back to my personal experiences with this understanding, I realized that in these situations, these people did not have self-awareness, nor were they empathetic. They themselves had a lot of personal issues. If anyone treats you horribly, realize it is not your problem *at all*.

4. Age Is Just a Number

For years I was insecure because of the bullying and I was the oldest in my grade. It made me anxious, but at the same time, I was the first one to get my license and the first one to turn twenty-one out of my friends. People were jealous I could do certain things first, although it didn't matter in the grand scheme of things. Age is just a number. It mattered to me for so long, but then I accepted it and took a step back and realized I was okay.

---

11   Caroline Bologna, "What Kids Who Bully Often Have in Common," *HuffPost*, August 30, 2019. Website News Article.

5. Go at Your Own Pace

Repeating a grade is not the end. It was supposed to help me—*and it did*. Having more time gave me more tools for success.

It's not a big deal to go at your own pace and not compete with anyone else. It is **okay** and **normal** not to be on the same page. One thing I've learned is that life is not a race. It is about going at your own speed. You do not need to be at the same speed as everyone else.

Driving is a perfect example of this. When you are driving a car, you worry about how fast you are going, not how everyone else around you is driving. You are going at your own speed. Yes, you want to drive the speed limit, but if you are on a highway and a car wants to pass you, let it. As long as you are going as fast as you need to go, do not worry about what everyone else around you is doing.

Jeremy Nicholson, M.S.W., Ph.D. says:

Why is it that we are so compelled to follow the crowd, even when it is objectively clear that they are wrong? According to more recent research, we may simply be wired that way. Specifically, these social influences can actually change our perceptions and memories (Edelson, Sharot, Dolan, & Dudai, 2011). Therefore, rather than knowingly making the wrong choice just to conform to peer pressure, the influence of others may actually change what we see as the correct choice in the moment and remember as the right thing after the fact. Beyond that, we might just have "herding brains" with built-in components that monitor our social alignments and make us feel good when we follow the crowd too." (Shamay-Tsoory, Saporta, Marton-Alper, & Gvirts, 2019). [12]

It isn't a bad thing to be your own person and not follow the crowd. Do what is best for you and your well-being. You do not need to worry about if you finish before or after someone else. Focus on the right time for YOU. This is your life. You only have one and you deserve to make the most of it.

How do you do you?

---

12 Jeremy Nicholson, Ph.D., "Should You Do What Everyone Else Is Doing?" *Psychology Today,* Sussex Publishers, March 31, 2019.

CHAPTER 2

Pressures of Society

———

Status: Position or rank in relation to others. [13]

Have you ever thought that maybe you are who society wants you to be and not who you actually want to be? Have you ever thought that if you did not act a certain way or do a certain thing you would not fit in? It is time to end the social norms. We all deserve to be true to ourselves.

Society starts brainwashing us from the moment we are born. We come into this world feeling surrounded by love. How can it change so quickly from love to hate as we grow up? **Society.** Society demands us to have a certain status or name. It allows us the right to treat people differently because of the assumption of being higher on the social status scale. These days it is common for people to use each other to get ahead, and that in turn adds fuel to the fire.

One outcome of social influence is the development of **social norms**—*the ways of thinking, feeling, or behaving that are*

———

13   *Merriam-Webster, s.v.* "status (n.)," accessed August 30, 2020.

shared by group members and perceived by them as appropriate *(Asch, 1955; Cialdini, 1993). Norms include customs, traditions, standards, and rules, as well as the general values of the group. Through norms, we learn what people actually do ("people in the United States are more likely to eat scrambled eggs in the morning and spaghetti in the evening, rather than vice versa") and also what we should do ("do unto others as you would have them do unto you") and shouldn't do ("do not make racist jokes"). There are norms about almost every possible social behavior, and these norms have a big influence on our actions.* [14]

There are some social norms designed to protect us and there are some that do the opposite, such as pressure from your peers to drink alcohol, do drugs, or have sex. Whatever it may be, social pressure is all around us no matter how old we are.

"Peer pressure is not just about kids. It happens in work environments, politics, sporting events. What do we do to address the factors that would lead towards conformity in ourselves when we may not even be aware of the influence?" [15]

Most of us are constantly trying to hold ourselves to a higher standard. I have definitely tried to do that in the past. We are always comparing ourselves to what we see is the best and then move on to the next. Next "like." Next picture. Next boyfriend/girlfriend. Next job. Next, next, next. And then

14   Rajiv Jhangiani, Hammond Tarry, and Charles Stangor, "Defining Social Psychology: History and Principles," *Principles of Social Psychology 1st International Edition,* September 26, 2014.

15   Derek A. Kreager and Jeremy Staff, "The Sexual Double Standard and Adolescent Peer Acceptance," *Social Psychology Quarterly,* June 1, 2009.

there is more. More views. More "likes." More comments. More people to validate us. Just more!

Compare and Compete? For What?

Society gave me the perspective I needed to be perfect in order to be beautiful. This impossible ideal perpetuated a negative experience for me as a teenager. I trusted the images I saw daily. If I was not skinny, did not have perfect skin or teeth, or you name it, I simply was not measuring up to society and its standards. I would strive for everything to be perfect because if I was, I would fit in. I destroyed myself in pursuit of society's approval and constantly tried to uphold a certain image; it was exhausting and left me drained and beyond broken inside.

One of the biggest factors to encouraging this perception for me was social media. I thought it was cool to have so many followers, "likes," and comments. I would see models and pictures of incredible places. I would scroll through my social media accounts and assume that each person out there had the perfect life. I thought "likes" were everything. These people had flawless lives because they were super popular. They had it all. Is that really the truth? Society has made it seem that social media is only good for posting the perfect moments. I was not living my life to my full potential when I would see these images all around me, prompting me to portray myself as someone I truly was not. I disrespected myself by allowing others to dictate how I should be, leaving me vulnerable to do anything for approval. I constantly altered who I was. I compromised my values and morals, which made me miserable because I was so insecure.

Society has become a place of incessantly comparing ourselves to each other, especially on social media, which promotes an opportunity to tear each other apart. It has gotten to the point where it is not **at all** healthy. We are losing people to suicide at a horrifying rate over how much we let this "idea" of the world affect us. Our mental health is becoming worse and worse. None of us look the way we do in edited pictures or magazines. "Perfect" is not real life. McLean Hospital states:

Facebook, Instagram, and Snapchat increase the likelihood of seeing unrealistic, filtered photos at a time when teen bodies are changing. In the past, teens read magazines that contained altered photos of models. Now, these images are one thumb-scroll away at any given time. Apps that provide the user with airbrushing, teeth whitening, and more filters are easy to find and easier to use. It's not only celebrities who look perfect—it's everyone. [16]

Sometimes the truth is not what people want to hear, or see, which can create a barrier that holds people back from being honest. My intention for writing this book is not to tell people how to live their lives. Rather, it is to show how our current culture has created an environment that has negatively impacted my life and the lives of many. I am expressing the emotional distress of this environment. Raising awareness is the foundation to making valuable and needed change. It is time to end this fake world.

---

16   "The Social Dilemma: Social Media and Your Mental Health," McLean Hospital, February 26, 2020.

Peace of Mind

I have never felt freer and more open to life than I did when I stopped giving a shit about anyone else's approval except my own. I will not compromise who I am anymore. Anyone who has something bad or unkind to say about you is likely just struggling within themselves. It has nothing to do with you. Brush it off and move forward. If anyone can relate, know that letting go of the fake you and freeing yourself from the toxic "perfection" idea is healthier in the long run.

I am happy with myself. I do not need anyone to make me happy. If I could go back and give my sixteen-year-old self some advice, it would be, *stop giving a shit about what others think of you; what matters is what you think of yourself.* If I could have done this, I might have found my confidence a lot sooner. However, I am living and learning like everybody else. Learning is a part of growing up.

Growing up can also include developing a different perspective of the world around you, a way to look beyond your own issues, and appreciate the struggles others may be facing. I used to think I needed to follow the common social norms to fit in and be liked. I never thought about changing my perspective. Instead, I constantly put pressure on myself and never took a break from it. Much of my depression spiraled out of control because of being narrow-minded, which gave me a skewed perception of life. I was not able to see the big picture. Once I opened up and allowed myself to heal, I realized I had control over how to live my life. I could make my own standards for what "society" should be for me. Why should I change myself for others? Being open-minded to this idea has been a turning point for me.

> **We are narrow-minded and dogmatic.** *If people were rational and open-minded, then the straightforward way to correct someone's false beliefs would be to present them with some relevant facts…It doesn't help that many of us are overconfident about how much we understand things and that, when we believe our opinions are superior to others, this deters us from seeking out further relevant knowledge.* [17]

Never in our lifetime have we been connected to the experiences and opinions of others as we currently are. COVID-19 has been a reality check for the world. No matter who we are or where we come from, we have all been affected by this terrible pandemic in a similar way. We have embraced the internet fully to stay connected. Social norms and social media are more profound and relevant now than they have ever been. Imagine if, by opening up our perception and compassion to the hardships we are all simultaneously experiencing, we could usher in change of our social norms for the better. What a great opportunity.

Status

Whether we are a "normal" person or a celebrity like Miley Cyrus, we are all fighting our own battles. Miley is a person just like us. Shocker, right? In a YouTube interview about her album *Plastic Hearts*, she talks about how she does not like the term "fans" or "audience" because she wants to break

---

17   Christian Jarrett, "The 10 Toxic Psychological Traits That Make So Many People Suck," *Fast Company*, December 11, 2018.

down that barrier and connect with people on a more personal level. She has been real with what she has gone through since being in the spotlight from a very young age. She has a voice and uses it to be open and honest, which is lacking in society because we are afraid to be looked down upon. It is mind-boggling to me that people judge other people's problems when it does not even concern them. These so-called ideals must go back to a time where we tried to establish rules for civilization to live freely without chaos. How do we know when we have gone too far? Who is responsible for correcting the course we are on?

We are.

The issue here is, as stated earlier, societal norms derived by social influence come from doing what others are doing. We learn what to do and what not to do based on the expectations of social norms and the actions of others. We are compelled to know the difference between right and wrong, and yet, as a society, sometimes we do not choose as wisely as we should. In Miley's interview, she talks about how so much is expected of society, and how no one truly talks to each other anymore. Music has always helped her. It is, however, important to take the time to dissect and come to the root of the issue because that is part of the problem. She said in the interview:

"We live in this society where we are just asked to compartmentalize, compartmentalize, compartmentalize." [18]

18   "Miley Cyrus—Apple Music *'Plastic Hearts'* Interview," interview by Zane Lowe, YouTube, November 23, 2020, video, 1:19:24.

Most of my teen life, I hid everything from the world and only showed what I thought people wanted to see. I let social platforms and media get into my head. I essentially ruined myself by doing that. The COVID-19 pandemic has been an opportunity to see life in a different light. Hopefully, this will help the world become more inclusive and less divisive. It is heartbreaking to see how many lives were taken during the pandemic. It made me appreciate my health so much more and not take it for granted. It made me appreciate what really is important. How awesome would it be if we all focused on what really matters in life?

Have you ever thought about why we long for "likes" and attention on social media anyway?

> *Neuroscientists are studying the effects of social media on the brain and finding that positive interactions (such as someone liking your tweet) trigger the same kind of chemical reaction that is caused by gambling and recreational drugs. According to an article by Harvard University researcher Trevor Haynes, when you get a social media notification, your brain sends a chemical messenger called dopamine along a reward pathway, which makes you feel good. Dopamine is associated with food, exercise, love, sex, gambling, drugs...and now, social media. Variable reward schedules up the ante; psychologist B.F. Skinner first described this in the 1930s. When rewards are delivered randomly (as with a slot machine or a positive interaction on social media), and checking for the reward is easy, the dopamine-triggering behavior becomes a habit.* [19]

---

19   Kelly McSweeney, "This is Your Brain on Instagram: Effects of Social Media on the Brain," *NOW*, March 17, 2019.

This is an explanation as to why we crave those likes. It is truly no different than an addiction. So, when something we don't want happens in our social media, or we get a negative comment, we get depressed.

Consider Instagram's implementation of a variable-ratio reward schedule. As explained in this 60 Minutes *interview, Instagram's notification algorithms will sometimes withhold "likes" on your photos to deliver them in larger bursts. When you make your post, you may be disappointed to find less responses than you expected, only to receive them in a larger bunch later on. Your dopamine centers have been primed by those initial negative outcomes to respond robustly to the sudden influx of social appraisal. This use of a variable reward schedule takes advantage of our dopamine-driven desire for social validation, and it optimizes the balance of negative and positive feedback signals until we've become habitual users.* [20]

Does anyone remember the days when we could have a conversation with someone without the distraction of technology or a cell phone? I do not. My parents talk about a time when it was easy to shut out the rest of the world, but now it is nearly impossible. Technology has created its own mental health dilemma.

Social media might be fueling the increase in mental illness, as Gen Z is the first truly digital generation. Pew Research Center found 45% of teens aged thirteen to seventeen said they use the internet "almost constantly." Over-use of social

---

20 Trevor Haynes, "Dopamine, Smartphones & You: A Battle for Your Time," (blog), Science in the News, Harvard University the Graduate School of Arts and Sciences, May 1, 2018, accessed January 10, 2021.

media can cause loneliness, depression, and anxiety, the
Anxiety and Depression Association of America reported. [21]

Double Standard?

During my years in college, I experienced a lot of double standards when it came to women versus men. Why can guys hook up with as many women as they want, but not the other way around? Double standards are wrong. It is stated that men are often praised for how many women they have slept with, and of course, we all know it is the opposite for women.

> *According to the sexual double standard, boys and men are rewarded and praised for heterosexual sexual contacts, whereas girls and women are derogated and stigmatized for similar behaviors...Results suggest that the association between lifetime sexual partnerships and peer status varies significantly by gender, such that greater numbers of sexual partners are positively correlated with boys' peer acceptance, but negatively correlated with girls' peer acceptance.* [22]

Lessons Learned

1. *Treat People the Way You Want to Be Treated*

No one should be able to discredit someone else because they might make less money or are less popular. It comes down

---

21 Andy Kiersz and Allana Akhtar, "Suicide is Gen Z's Second-leading Cause of Death, and It's a Worse Epidemic Than Anything Millennials Faced at That Age," *Business Insider*, October 17, 2019.

22 Derek A. Kreager and Jeremy Staff, "The Sexual Double Standard and Adolescent Peer Acceptance," *Social Psychology Quarterly*, June 1, 2009.

to asking yourself, how would you feel if someone dismissed or disrespected you?

2. *"Likes" and Comments Are Not the All Be-All and End-All*

Everyone wants feedback on whatever they post. I sure do, but I do not let that control my life. "Likes" and comments have no reflection on anyone's character and who they are. Post what you want, as long as you are not hurting someone else. Who cares if someone likes it or not? I now ask myself, "Do *I* like it?" If I do, then I post it. Never get down on yourself about social media. It is supposed to be fun and not overused.

3. *Double Standard Goodbye*

The only way life should be lived is how you want to live it. It is as simple as this: I live my life the way I want, and I want you to do the same. We don't need to call women terrible things when men are doing the same thing. Peer acceptance should not be based on the number of people with whom someone sleeps.

4. *Be Open-Minded*

I was narrow-minded for years. I was very closed off and not open to new perspectives; however, when I put myself in someone else's shoes, I become more sympathetic. Regardless, be respectful if someone does not think the same as you do. We all are entitled to our opinions. It makes the world interesting.

5. Value Where Other People Are

I learned many lessons during the pandemic, but the biggest one was to appreciate what someone else is going through. Each of us is important. Don't forget that you are worth it, no matter what. Regardless of what pressures society throws at us, we are all valuable.

Next time you find yourself making an assumption about someone else, take a step back and ask yourself:

Is it kind?

Is it how I would like to be treated?

How would I feel if it were me?

CHAPTER 3

Different or Unique?

Learning Disability: Any of various conditions (such as dyslexia or dysgraphia) that interfere with an individual's ability to learn and so result in impaired functioning in language, reasoning, or academic skills (such as reading, writing, and mathematics) and that are thought to be caused by difficulties in processing and integrating information—called also learning difference. [23]

I felt "different" daily. I always worked hard in school but it took me twice as long to learn the same thing as everyone else. I never felt that I fit in. I felt completely different from my peers. I was never like them. I could not accept that I was different and instead felt ashamed and incompatible to the world.

From the very beginning I have felt that no matter what I did, I was always misunderstood. I felt lost and had an abundance of depression that never wanted to fade away. Instead, it persisted in my life and led to anxiety. Constantly, I felt that no one wanted to be around me because I was

---

23 *Merriam-Webster, s.v.* "learning disability (n.)," accessed September 14, 2020.

different or would say the wrong thing. I never raised my hand or talked to people because I was too timid and shy. I never embraced myself for who I was. I wanted to be the same as everyone else. Because I was not and I could not figure out why, I became lost and broken. I didn't let myself live because I constantly worried about being separate from everyone else. A lot of my depression began after the bullying I experienced as a child. I felt that no one could relate to what I was going through and I saw myself as nothing. My freshman year of high school was the start to a new level of darkness for me. Lonely days only continued to get worse in my sophomore year.

"Live your life for you, not for anyone else. Don't let the fear of being judged, rejected, or disliked stop you from being yourself."

~SONYA PARKER

The reality is, adolescent depression is a serious problem. The 2001-2004 National Comorbidity Survey: Adolescent Supplement of 10,123 adolescents found that 11% of teens suffer with major depressive disorder by age eighteen. More recently, the US National Institute of Mental Health found that 2.7 million adolescents ages twelve to seventeen (10.7% of all adolescents) suffered a major depressive episode in 2013. If depression is left untreated, the intense feelings of sadness, hopelessness, anger, or frustration can last for weeks, months, or years. The World Health Organization reports that worldwide, over 350 million people suffer from depression, making it the leading cause of disability and contributor to the overall global burden of disease. It is critical to recognize symptoms of depression to make early treatment possible and prevent pain, suffering, and possible death. [24]

"We need to talk to you."

Two words. Boarding. School.

One day during my sophomore year of high school, I went to a doctor's office and was asked to do a few assessment tests. A few weeks later, my parents and I had a meeting in our family room. I walked in and my mom said, "We need to talk to you. I have something I need to share. We've found something out from the tests you took and we need to look into it further. It's something that should help you."

I screamed, "What now?"

She continued with, "Remember how you always struggle in math and science, but you are good at reading and writing? Well honey, you know how we had you take those tests at the doctor's office a few weeks ago? The doctor has diagnosed you with a learning disability which is called "nonverbal learning disability." Your dad and I think its best if we look at other educational options. We found a few boarding schools in New England that could really help you."

I was shocked. I never thought I would hear that in my life. I thought, "Am I stupider than everyone else? Is this why I am so different?" When I first found out I had a learning

---

24 Michael Shulman, "One in Three College Freshmen Worldwide Reports Mental Health Disorder," American Psychological Association, September 13, 2018, accessed September 13, 2020.

disability, I was in disbelief. I was shocked and in denial. I didn't take it well. I felt stupid and alone. I felt defeated. It took me a while to realize that having a learning disability did not define me. It never made me any less of a person. It made me realize that, if anything, it has made me more of who I am, and the "difference" was something to embrace.

Children with NLD have difficulties understanding nonverbal information, which can result in academic, social, and emotional challenges. Contrary to the name of this disorder, these children often have excellent verbal skills and do well in elementary school, delaying detection of their learning disability. Their academic problems come to light as school becomes more complex and implied learning replaces rote learning. [25]

Still Smart, Just Different

Any disability, especially a nonverbal learning disability, isn't a frailty. It's a *difference*. It is so important for anyone who has one now or discovers one later to not beat themselves up about it. Yes, I did have to take remedial math freshmen year (before I knew I had NLD) when I was in public school and did not know why. However, I see clearly now that it was not a strength of mine. Math is not, nor will it ever be, my thing. I do know the struggles faced when dealing with a learning disability. It is something that needs to be embraced by all schools because not all of us learn the same way and that is okay.

---

25 "Nonverbal Learning Disabilities: An Overview," Smart Kids with Learning Disabilities, accessed February 1, 2021.

While there are some negatives to having a learning difference, I do not focus on those. I have learned that focusing on the good in a situation can make life so much better. It is my hope that others with learning disabilities can see their own potential as well, because we all have it inside of us. It's about bringing your inner self to the surface.

I have a dream to open an "Unbreakable" foundation to help people and hopefully save lives. I'd like to encourage that different is *good*. Different is life. Different is what sets us apart from each other and makes life interesting.

If you are not familiar with what nonverbal learning disability is, I would not be surprised. Many people do not, and that is okay. Basically, I am highly verbal, which makes sense because I love to talk (hello TED Talk: Never Say Never). In my life, socially, I usually take situations more personally than others, so with that I sometimes have a harder time letting things go. As far as how I was affected in school, it came down to my having to work harder than everyone else for above-average results. It affected me with almost all subjects, especially math and science.

> *Nonverbal Learning Disability describes a well-defined profile that includes strengths in verbal abilities contrasted with deficits in visual-spatial abilities. Individuals with NVLD often have trouble with some of the following: organization, attention, executive functioning, nonverbal communication, and motor skills.* [26]

---

26 "What is Nonverbal Learning Disability?" The NVLD Project | Nonverbal Learning Disability, accessed September 13, 2020.

The New Girl

Being someone who has gone to boarding school, I often got questions: "What did you do? Why did your parents ship you away?" No, my parents didn't "ship me away." They love me immensely. We all wish I could have stayed home. Ultimately, the hardest decision is sometimes the right decision. The most common misconception is that some people think only "bad" kids go to boarding school. That is false. According to boardingschools.com:

> *FAQ one: Isn't boarding school for kids who are in trouble? Boarding school is for students who are looking for more. Students who attend boarding school are usually among the most successful students at their home schools or are students who truly want to experience greater challenges.* [27]

The boarding school I attended was for kids with learning differences, especially dyslexia. Everyone who attended my boarding school learned differently and needed more attention (which is not a bad thing). Most of the people at my school had known about their learning disability for a while, so they did not have to deal with the initial shock I went through. Coincidentally, the day I toured the school, I met a girl who would become one of my very best friends. When I walked into the office to take the tour, she was there because she was moving in and starting that day.

---

[27] "The Big Picture on Boarding Schools," The Association of Boarding Schools, Accessed September 14, 2020.

Coming into this experience, the attention I got at first from being the new girl was overwhelming. I abruptly got a lot of social media attention. People started asking for my number. Guys thought I was "hot," which confused me. The first day I walked into the dining hall with my roommate, I am not kidding you when I say, everyone there stopped what they were doing and just stared. I mean *stared*. It was as if a bunch of piranhas had come to attack me. It was such a weird feeling. For the first time, I was getting attention. Everyone wanted to talk to me, and it was overwhelming. The attention from being the new girl lasted for quite a while and I was happy when it stopped. It felt like I was a celebrity, and I was just trying to live my life. It made me uncomfortable to be the new girl and the center of attention.

There was one guy whom I thought was really good-looking. I thought, "*Oh, he is hot. Damn, I will be fine here.*" Having people be nice to me was a new feeling.

Having a roommate was a big adjustment for me since I had my own room at home. My sophomore year roommate and I laugh now because when I first moved in, after a few days, we hated each other. We were just being immature and petty; now, we look back and laugh because we cannot even remember why. It probably had something to do with us both being used to having our own space and not used to rooming with someone else.

Now, fast forward to my junior year. I had a boyfriend. He was someone no one would have guessed I would have dated. He was a nice guy. He accepted me for who I was. It was a good first relationship even though it did not work out in the end. However, I wish him the best. I look back now and think about if I never would have gone there, I never would have met these amazing people who are some of my friends.

"Learning disabilities are not a prescription for failure. With the right kinds of instruction, guidance, and support, there are no limits to what individuals with LD can achieve." [28]

Life has its hard moments. That is a fact of life. Boarding school life and dating life is not how people expect it to be. We had Wednesday and Saturday half-day classes with every other weekday as a normal full day. After school, my day consisted of being involved in some sort of activity. After that, I would go to dinner and then study hall. Doing this over and over again and missing home was tough to the say the least. Regardless, it did bring me some of my closest friends and the bond we made at boarding school is permanent.

One of my friends was two years younger than me. I was a junior and she was a freshman. We were this unstoppable duo that did not care what people thought. We had a lot of fun together. We were up for new adventures and meeting new people. During fall semester, we had the opportunity to do a sport together, so we decided to do volleyball. We were not exactly good, nor a favorite of our coaches; there were so many girls, they had to create two JV teams. There was the JVA team of people who could actually play and

---

28 Candace Cortiella and Sheldon H. Horowitz, *The State of Learning Disabilities: Facts, Trends, and Emerging Issues,* New York: National Center for Learning Disabilities, 2014: 3, accessed September 13, 2020.

then the lovely JVB team. She and I were obviously on the JVB team. We thought it was so funny and laughed and had a good time. We even skipped practice a few times (I know, we were rebels).

During volleyball one day, she looked over to me and said, "Want to order a pizza?" I was hungry, so I said, "Yeah, of course. Let's do it." In the middle of practice, she got out her phone and ordered a pizza to the gym. Once it came, we moved over to the side of the gym and ate. Our coach looked over and was mad. She said something along the lines of, "Why aren't you taking this seriously?" My friend replied in a sassy way and said, "Um, its JVB?" Our coach gave up on us after that. Safe to say we were not high on her list.

Lessons Learned

1. *Different is Good*

The point of life is to be *different*. We are all unique and deserve to be who we are without getting any judgment. By constantly trying to be the same as everybody else, we are not letting ourselves truly embrace who we are and living life to the fullest.

2. *It Is Not a Disability. It Is a Difference*

Learning disabilities shouldn't be called "learning disabilities" because they are "learning differences." I am so much happier now that I embrace myself for everything I am. Truthfully, learning differences are more common than most people realize.

One in five children in the US have learning and attention issues such as dyslexia and ADHD, but as noted in the new **State of Learning Disabilities: Understanding the 1 in 5** *(www.ncld.org/StateofLD), 48 percent of parents believe incorrectly that children will outgrow these brain-based difficulties, and 33 percent of educators say that sometimes what people call a learning disability is really just laziness.*[29]

3. High School Is High School Anywhere

High school is a hard phase of life. That is the reality. When I was a teenager, I was trying to figure out who I was supposed to be and not who I actually was and wanted to be. I sacrificed myself to fake it. "Fake it until you make it" gets you nowhere. It is about taking the time to learn about *you* and do whatever it is that makes you happy. The teenage years are tough and that is a fact. It is about making the most of it and, most importantly, getting through it.

4. Learning "Disabilities" Can Be a Blessing in Disguise

If you find out you have a learning "disability," remember you have strengths that make you special. Having smaller classes is what worked better for me when I was in school. I was not "dumb" and I needed to stop telling myself I was. I needed extra attention and that was okay. I learned the way that was best for me academically. I think differently. We are all our own unique individual self.

---

29   "The State of LD: Understanding the 1 in 5," National Center for Learning Disabilities, May 2, 2017, accessed January 10, 2021.

Dyslexia/ADD specialist and leader of Renaissance Mind Learning Facility, Angela Gonzales, MD, explains that often the traditional academic environment does not suit a non-traditional learner, but children with learning disabilities have a style of thinking that is a gift later on in life. She says, "These are highly visual, spatial, and conceptual learners that have the ability to distort perception and perceive it as reality. That's a problem in school, but in the real world, this style of thinking allows you to be a Lego builder extraordinaire. It allows you to be an artist. As you get older, it allows you to be the best architect, movie producer, musician, actor you can be. [30]

5. Changing One Variable Can Change Your Life

The change made in my life was that I was taken out of one school, where I was not doing well academically, and went somewhere else where I was set up on a path for success. All it takes is one "different" step in your life to direct you to a completely changed path. Denying your issues and keeping them to yourself does not help you at all. It becomes worse in the end.

What is something you can do "differently" in your life to better yourself?

How are some ways you learn differently?

---

30 Leana Greene, "Overcoming the Same of My Learning Disability," *Kids in the House* (blog), *Huffpost*, updated December 6, 2017.

CHAPTER 4

Life is a Blur

———

Isolate: To set apart from others; also: quarantine. [31]

*Life has its tough moments, but it also has those moments that take your breath away. Those are the moments that make life worth it. No matter what you believe, find some-thing to believe in. That is the point of life. There is **always** something ahead for you to believe in. For me, that was faith in God. Whatever it is for you, no matter what you believe in, **believe in it!***

Very early on in my college experience, I realized I was not the typical college girl. I didn't want to go out and get drunk every weekend. I didn't want to leave a party and go home with someone. I felt lost and alone trying to figure out where I fit in. I was sad every day and did not even know why I was alive or what my purpose was. It was not long after classes started when I started losing more and more of myself. I lost any confidence I had. I felt broken, alone, and barely there each day. Each week only got worse with classes becoming

---

31 *Merriam-Webster, s.v.* "isolate (v.)." accessed September 10, 2020.

more difficult. Getting through my classes with depression and anxiety was a huge challenge. I was a time bomb that could go off at any second.

According to the American College Health Association Fall 2018 National College Health Assessment, 63 percent of college students in the US felt overwhelming anxiety in the past year. In the same survey, 23 percent reported being diagnosed or treated by a mental health professional for anxiety in the past year. The sharpest increase in anxiety occurs during the initial transition to college. A recent study demonstrated that psychological distress among college students — that is, their levels of anxiety, depression, and stress — rises steadily during the first semester of college and remains elevated throughout the second semester. This suggests that the first year of college is an especially high-risk time for the onset or worsening of anxiety. [32]

A few weeks into the first semester I knew I had made a mistake. It got to the point where my parents wanted to pull me out of school in the middle of the semester. Just having that conversation was difficult. If that would have happened, none of my current credits would transfer to another school since I would not finish my classes. It would mean I would have to start at the beginning again, so we decided I would finish out the semester. In the midst of my downward spiral, I did apply to a school back home and got accepted for the second semester.

---

32   Nicole J. LeBlanc, M.A. and Luana Marques, Ph.D., "Anxiety in College: What We Know and How to Cope," *Harvard Health Blog,* (blog), Harvard Health Publishing, May 28, 2019.

Walking back to my dorm room after class was taxing to say the least. Every day I had the same routine: after class, I stopped to get an Einstein's bagel and strawberry smoothie before walking back to my dorm, only to be isolated and sad in my room again. Day after day, class after class, I would be back in my room and on my twin bed. Usually, I would start crying because this was the same routine and it made me feel as lonely as ever. I would grab my computer and turn on *New Girl.* I would watch it for the rest of the night, not leaving my room except to shower. My depression got so bad that I would go home every weekend. That was basically the only other time I would leave my room.

My mom would drive up every Friday (best mom, seriously) to take me home. I was stuck with weeks to go to finish the first semester before I would be able to be back home for good. Even though there was an end in sight, I could not see it. I still had no one to go to meals with or hang with at school. I was so depressed that my appetite became nonexistent. When my mom would pick me up, she would bring me Chipotle to eat in the car. I was so depressed I could barely eat it, and it was one of my favorites. This was when she and the rest of my family became alarmed.

> *"Loss of appetite can be an early sign of depression or a warning of a depression relapse. On the other hand, some people can't stop eating when they are depressed," says Gary Kennedy, MD, director of geriatric psychiatry at Montefiore Medical Center in Bronx, New York. "A sudden change in weight, either gaining or losing, can be a warning of depression,*

especially in someone who has other symptoms of depression
or a history of depression." [33]

In addition to my loneliness and depression, I was also facing roommate issues. I think the reason had something to do with her getting up at four a.m. every morning for ROTC. It was not long before she moved out, and I had to face another scary reality. I had an empty bed sitting across from me, and it reminded me of how empty I was inside. It was mid-October, and I was running out of options—or so I thought. I felt so isolated that I started to self-harm almost every day. I had no will to live. I became numb to emotions and feelings and felt that no matter what I did, I just did not matter to anyone. I felt no one saw me or heard me. I was getting to the point where I was actively thinking about ending the pain I had felt for so many years. I hit rock bottom.

Life felt absolutely unbearable. I thought I could end the struggles I constantly faced. Everyone would move on with their lives and forget me because I did not feel needed, wanted, or a part of anything. I felt that this was it, and there was nothing for me to live for anymore. I was useless and worthless. One fall night, I came back to my dorm room. Feeling melancholy like always, I sat on my bed, eating a bagel, drinking a smoothie, and watching Netflix. It was the same thing every day and nothing changed.

Don't get me wrong—of course I wished for my life to get better, but that was not happening. I struggled to get through

---

33   Chris Iliades, M.D., "Depression's Effect on Your Appetite," *Everyday Health*, September 10, 2012.

each day. The days went by way too slowly. At this point my mental health deteriorated even more.

The Washington Post has done research about the mental health of college freshmen.

More than one of every three college freshmen across the globe—35 percent—show symptoms of one of the common mental-health disorders, according to new research published by the American Psychological Association. The research was based on World Health Organization data on 13,984 full-time freshman students from 19 colleges in eight countries — Australia, Belgium, Germany, Mexico, Northern Ireland, South Africa, Spain, and the United States. The two most common disorders found were major depression (affecting 21 percent of the students) and generalized anxiety disorder (19 percent). [34]

After all the horrible things I used to hear, like how I should kill myself, "Marvin the Martian," and getting unasked to *multiple* dances, being rejected and betrayed by so many hit me all at once. Feeling like a loser with no friends came flooding into my brain, and I could not take it. In a split second, it felt as though an avalanche of bricks had hit me.

Trigger Warning: This section contains a description of attempted suicide. Please don't read if it will trigger you.

I had a million thoughts enter my head telling me how much people did not like me. How worthless I was. How nobody

---

34 Linda Searing, "The Big Number: 1 in 3 College Freshmen Show Signs of Mental Health Disorders," *The Washington Post*, WP Company, September 25, 2018.

loved me. How I was not good enough. I did not feel I was needed anymore. I wondered if they thought I was ugly? Do they think I am annoying? What the fuck is so wrong with me? Why don't I fit in? Why do I suck so much?

I saw myself as worthless, useless, a burden, stupid, ugly, alone, a reject, and a loser.

My stomach was in knots. I started shaking and felt like I could not live another day. I had no idea why I was still alive. I was already having a terrible night and suddenly I lost my shit. I was lying on my bed, crying my eyes out, when I saw something on my dresser that could be the solution to end my pain *forever*. I might have just found the answer to my problem. As fucked up as it sounds, I was so excited. I had just discovered the answer: overdose.

Suddenly a rush of chills went through my whole body. Still bawling my eyes out, I got out of bed and went over to the brown dresser that dorms provide. I looked down at my little plastic drawers I used for my makeup. The bottom drawer is where I kept my medications. I reached in and put the pills on the top of the dresser. I then opened the top drawer, because I had a bottle of Advil. I picked it up and placed it next to the other pill bottles. I stood there picking up each one. I knew if I combined everything together, I would die in about five minutes. All I had to do...

My head then went into a blank space. I had no idea what I was doing anymore. I just knew that I could be gone in five minutes if I did this right. Then terrible thoughts about myself started spinning in my head again. I thought, oh, they will get *over this. They do not need me. I do not need this life anymore. I suck. No one will ever love me. My head began to spin and I got dizzy. I was crying heavily and then thought, "This is it. I am about to end all of my pain once and for all."*

Please Stay, I Need You

I had all the pills on the dresser. Staring at them, I started to hyperventilate. "Just do it," I thought. "Take ten or twelve or the entire bottle and I will be gone. That's it. That is all it takes." My whole body was shaking at this point and I did not know what was going on. I felt that if I could just do this as quickly as possible, I could take my useless self out of the world and make it a better place for everyone I knew. I know now that that thought is NOT true at all. I would have made their lives worse.

I had people who loved me. I had a few friends back home and my family. I was not thinking about them at all. The only thing I thought about was the number of pills I needed to take to make sure I was planning it out right so I would be dead. When in such a hyperactive state, it was hard to pull myself back to reality. It is really important in that state to not be super impulsive; had I been even more impulsive, I would be gone.

The truth is more college students struggle with this than most would think. According to the American Psychological Association, it states:

> *As if college were not difficult enough, more than one-third of first-year university students in eight industrialized countries around the globe report symptoms consistent with a*

diagnosable mental health disorder, according to research published by the American Psychological Association. [35]

My hands felt numb at this point and my body was shaking. I wanted to do the "easy" fix and overdose.

I started to pour out maybe six or seven pills into my hand. I looked at the amount I had and thought I needed all of it to make it work. I dumped the entire bottle into my hand. I was looking at the pills thinking I was so close to getting out of this terrible depression. I was so close. This was all I had to do. I didn't have to struggle again.

I stopped for a second and decided to open the bottle of the pills I had by my other hand. If I dumped as many pills as I could into my hands, I would for sure be gone. I just had to make sure I took enough. Stop talking about it just do it. It takes a second and this will be the end. I had one hand with the pills in them and the other held the empty bottle.

You are about to overdose, and all your pain will be taken away.

Would my pain really have been taken away?

Young people are dying from suicide at record rates. The suicide rate among people aged ten to twenty-four increased 56 percent between 2007 and 2017, according to a new report by the Centers for Disease Control and Prevention…Suicide

---

35 American Psychological Association, "One in Three College Freshmen Worldwide Reports Mental Health Disorder," American Psychological Association, September 13, 2018, accessed September 13, 2020.

was the second-leading cause of death for people aged ten to twenty-four in 2017. [36]

I slowly raised the pills up three inches away from my mouth. I was breathing so heavily and frantically. I cried hysterically and hyperventilated. I felt so dizzy I could barely breathe. I opened my mouth.

Just then my phone started vibrating. I put the pills down slowly and walked back to my bed where I had left my phone. I turned the phone over in order to press "ignore," but then I saw who it was. It was **my best friend.**

I thought to myself, Well, I can at least say bye to her and tell her I can't do this anymore. I picked up crying into the phone. I said, "No. No. I need to go. Stop. Bye—it's just not worth it anymore. I can't do it anymore. Bye—"

She completely cut me off.

"WHAT? Carolyn? Carolyn? You're not okay. What is going on? Please talk to me."

I said, "I need to die. I love you. I just can't anymore. You know I have never and will never fit in. I am done. These pills are the ans—"

---

36   Andy Kiersz and Allana Akhtar, "Suicide is Gen Z's Second-Leading Cause of Death and It's a Worse Epidemic Than Anything Millennials Faced at That Age," *Business Insider*, October 17, 2019.

Crying. Cutting me off, she screamed, "Put those pills back in the bottle right now! Carolyn, I swear to God, don't you dare do anything. NOTHING! Put them back NOW!"

"If you think a loved one is thinking about or planning suicide, ask. It's a myth that you'll give another person the idea to kill him or herself. Asking shows that you're concerned and that you care about the person." [37]

Still hysterical, I said, "No, just let me do something. I gotta do it. It's time. I love you but I am done. I have never fit in, and I never will. There is no hope. I fucking hate my life. Good—"

Again she cut me off, screaming, "CAROLYN! You better keep me on the phone. I am not hanging up and neither are you. You are not hanging up. No. I swear, Carolyn. Please."

I found out later that she was the one who made the closest people in my life aware. She texted my mom and another friend while she was talking to me.

I was crying, trying to fight her by saying, "What the fuck? Why are you telling my family and our friends? Like, no, just let me die. I can't. Really. I can't go on. I am beyond broken and fucked up. There is no hope. I am done. Please just let me go."

Yelling this time, she demanded I stay on the phone and cut me off again.

---

37 Marcia Purse, "What is Suicidal Ideation? A Look at Dangerous Thought Patterns," *Very Well Mind*, Dotdash, March 25, 2020.

"No. No! Carolyn! Carolyn, listen to me. You are going to get through this. I promise you I am by your side, and I'm never going to leave. I will always be here but stay on the fucking phone! Don't even think of hanging up. I swear—you better not even think about hanging up, I swear. They need to know what is going on. I am going to help you through this. Your parents and professionals will, too. You will get better, Carolyn. Believe me, please!" she said as her voice began to shake.

I still was not having it, so I said, "No! No one should know. I am ashamed. Why the fuck is this my life? Please, just let me."

I tried to fight with her a little bit more and then she said something that, for some reason, got me to listen to her for a minute. I really have no idea how, yet she did.

She went on. "There is nothing to be ashamed about. We—me, your parents, your sister, your friends at home—we are here for you. You have to, and you will get through this. There is nothing wrong with not being okay, but you really need to get help for it. I promise this will be good for you in the end. Please don't. I can't lose you. You're my best friend. I love you. Please!" Her voice cracked.

Suddenly, I stopped. I heard the distress in her voice. I heard how scared she was to lose me. Subconsciously, I heard her. She said **best friend.** I was someone's best friend. I mattered and meant something to her—and not just her. I mattered. I had something greater to offer the world. I had someone who saw I was worth it and that I had so much more going for me in my life. While I was in a crisis, panic, suicidal mode, I had no idea what I could have done to myself. Even if I did survive an "attempt," the amount of health problems I could have faced would have had astronomical consequences.

> When people survive a self-poisoning suicide attempt, they may have heart problems or seizures afterwards. [John] Ackerman, [Suicide Prevention Coordinator at the Center for Suicide Prevention and Research at Nationwide Children's Hospital in Columbus, Ohio] said that the drugs may have an impact on brain function as well. "This paper is a call to action for parents to increase their safe storage practices and talk to kids about their mental health concerns," he added. "Ask your kids how they're doing." Parents may think it's impossible to keep kids away from all medicines. "But, if you're adding barriers—like a lock box or safe, and counting medication—those seemingly simple tasks can help. They can be a bridge to a child or teen seeing other options," Ackerman explained. [38]

I was still on the phone with her and tried to fight back so she would leave me alone and just let me die. I told her this was not something she could fix. I continued saying, "Please stop. There is nothing you can do. I am hopeless. I suck. I love you, but I need to do this."

She was, of course, bawling her eyes out by now, and I was unbearably beside myself. I could barely catch my breath. I then heard my phone ding and saw a ton of texts. Many were from my parents and friends back home. I started getting calls, but ignored them, since I was only talking to her.

---

38 Serena Gordon, "Kids Often Use OTC Drugs in Suicide Attempts," WebMD Archives, originally published by HealthDay News, October 7, 2019.

My Best Friend, My Saving Grace

Somehow, some way, this miraculous friend got me to calm down. I do not know how she did it when I was that hysterical. She is an incredible person and is always there for me. **She saved my life.** She stopped me from doing something that would have absolutely torn out so many loved ones' hearts and would have been the **biggest mistake of my life.** I was incredibly lucky to have a person there. Unfortunately, not everyone does. Our stories are not supposed to end on our account. I would have ended my story way too soon and missed out on so many great things. Luckily, I had her: my absolute saving grace.

She knows who she is. She is a smart, independent, funny, nice, amazing, beautiful person inside and out. She is *herself*, which is amazing. She will not settle. She holds herself with grace and respect. She is the kind of person everyone needs in their life. Her energy is contagious and we have the most fun adventures together. There is no one else I would rather blast Dan and Shay or Taylor Swift with. In all honesty, she truly is the best friend I have ever had. She and her family are amazing people. She doesn't like to get all sappy and emotional. We have grown so much together. When she reads this, I hope she knows I will always be by her side, just as she has always been there for me. She pushes me in a good way. She pushed me away from suicide and I can never repay her for that. She is my forever angel and will always occupy a deep place in my heart. She pushes me to be a better version of myself.

Thank you. I love you.

You Are Never Alone

If you are in the middle of the chaos and think you should end your life, please realize that the chaos is really a small fragment of your life. It will pass! There is so much more to see and live for. I am beyond thankful I did not take those pills that night. There is no other me, like there is no other you. You are valuable. Others need you. If you are in a low point right now and think it's a good idea, you are wrong. It will destroy so many people who love you by taking away the most precious thing of all: **you**. You will leave the biggest hole in everyone's heart. Everyone who loves you will be devastated. Even if you think no one cares, you are **wrong**. You are cared for and loved more than you think. Just make sure you try to see it, too. I understand the feeling of being unable to bear the world, but still there is hope at the end of the tunnel if you give yourself the chance to see it. Let yourself have that chance to rethink, to re-evaluate before you make a permanent decision. Seek help! Talk to someone. See the resource information at the end of this chapter.

Lessons Learned

1. *College Is Not the Best Four Years for Everyone*

I have heard plenty of times that "college is the best four years of your life." While that might be true for some, that was not true for me. Now, don't get me wrong, college did bring some amazing people into my life, but it also brought some hardships I had to get through. These hardships have made me stronger and more resilient.

2. *You Are NEVER Alone*

Reach out to get help if needed. No matter who you are, there is no shame in needing help. If you are ever in a crisis, call the number listed at the end of this chapter. Help is okay. You will come out on the other side, I promise you. It is all about buying into the help. It is so worth it. Never end your life. Please! You have so much more to live for. Life is worth the fight because what comes out of the fight is a stronger you.

3. *Find Someone to Confide in*

Having a lot of friends is not important. What is important is quality over quantity. Having even one best friend can truly change your whole world. Whether it is a therapist, friend, mom, dad, boyfriend, or girlfriend, find someone whom you can talk to.

4. *Never End Your Life on Your Account*

If there was one thing I could say to the people who love me the most it is, *I am sorry.* I am sorry for almost leaving them and making them live without me. I had and have way more to live for—and you do as well.

5. *Use Your Voice*

I am not in a perfect place in life; however, I am at a point where I think it is so important that everyone feel heard. Using my voice and writing this book did it for me. I came across a story by *Good Morning America* about attempted suicide survivors. I read this quote and it is important for everyone to remember none of us is alone.

"Since my attempt, I realized I had to learn how to give myself and others love, light, softness, and care. I have made a conscious effort to give voice to my pain and my struggles—in therapy and with friends—and through that I have learned I am not alone." [39]

Check in with yourself. Ask yourself: how am I actually doing?

Resources

In the US: Call the National Suicide Prevention Lifeline at 1-800-273-TALK (8255) or IMAlive at 1-800-784-2433.

The Trevor Project offers suicide prevention services for LGBTQ youth at **1-866-488-7386.**

SAMHSA's National Helpline offers referrals for substance abuse and mental health treatment at **1-800-662-4357.**

In the UK and Ireland: Call Samaritans UK at 116 123.

In Australia: Call Lifeline Australia at 13 11 14.

In other countries: Visit IASP or suicide.org to find a helpline in your country.

---

39 Katie Kindelan, "On World Suicide Prevention Day, What 4 Survivors of Suicide Want You to Know," Good Morning America, September 9, 2019.

PART 2

CHAPTER 5

The Pain Left Behind

Purpose: Something set up as an object or end to be attained: intention. [40]

*Suicide was almost my reality. A reality without me would have torn up so many people I know and love; their hearts shredded. Not only that, I would have left behind so much sadness and despair. I would have left the most loving, thoughtful, incredible, caring, and selfless person I have ever met: my mom. I thank God for letting me live and giving me her as my mother. I am blessed to have a great relationship with my mom, as well as my whole family, and that would not have been possible had I taken my own life. My mother. My family. My friends. I cannot even imagine what I would have done to all of them. All I know is I am here and **life is worth living**.*

Even though I almost gave up on my life, my heart knew I had so much more love to give, even if it was not apparent then. Life is a beautiful thing. Sometimes it is about pure trust and

---

40 Merriam-Webster, s.v. "purpose (n.)," accessed September 15, 2020.

having something to believe in. For me, it was God. I have always said I am Christian, but I was not fully a Christian until I gave my life to God completely and stopped trying to take hold of my life alone. When I was younger, I heard being a Christian meant "giving your life to God," and I never knew what that meant.

One day I prayed and prayed, "God I can't do this anymore. I can't live this life in this way. If you're up there, I need you. Please. I don't want to feel this way. I am tearing my family apart. I need help. Please."

Faith is something I hold onto and is something I believe in. Whatever you personally believe, it is all about trusting in something. I was looking for something. I did not know what I was searching for, but I realized in due time that God was answering my prayers.

Trust that life will work out because it is never worth giving up. Giving up on your life affects so many people around you. Recently, I was at a funeral for someone I knew who committed suicide. It tore my heart into pieces. I was devastated for the family. I was thinking, "*That was almost me.*" Seeing how heartbroken the family was, I just wanted to hug them all and tell them it was going to be okay.

After the funeral, I got in the car and bawled my eyes out. I asked my mom what she would have done "if." She just looked at me and said one word: "indescribable." She said she couldn't even think about it. She was beyond thankful I was still here. That is the truth. When someone takes their own life, they leave their loved ones heartbroken. Addressing mental health issues is essential.

> *It takes strength and persistence to recover from mental illness—to keep fighting symptoms in the hopes of feeling better. Even if you feel weak or powerless against the battles you face every day, you are incredibly strong for living through them. Practical and simple methods can help you in your fight. Take these techniques into consideration, and there will be a clear change in the way you feel and live your life.* [41]

My dad used to say to me, "One hour at a time." One hour, then the next. It is all about taking life one step at a time. It helps tremendously to reduce stress with daily life by simply taking a step back. I have learned it is important to understand why I was anxious and depressed. Once I figured out where the root of my issues were coming from, I could address the situation and find the solution. When I figured out what was causing my agony and sadness, I was then able to take the necessary steps toward finding a solution and becoming less stressed. The cause of depression can help with the treatment and care needed.

> *Understanding the underlying cause of your depression may help you overcome the problem. For example, if you are depressed because of a dead-end job, the best treatment might be finding a more satisfying career rather than simply taking an antidepressant. If you are new to an area and*

---

41 Emmie Pombo, "Self-Help Techniques for Coping with Mental Illness," National Alliance on Mental Illness, February 1, 2019.

eling lonely and sad, finding new friends will probably give
you more of a mood boost than going to therapy. In such
cases, the depression is remedied by changing the situation. [42]

Whenever suicide happens, the people behind are left in complete despair. I realize now that I would have left my family in distress and even worse, I would have been gone forever. I would have hurt so many people, and you would, too. I could not explain to you how many people have impacted my life for the better to help me get out of the dark storm I was facing. I was honestly so broken, so inexplicably miserable day in and out until I found something worth believing in.

You Are Never Alone

Whatever you may be facing right now is temporary. You know what is not? **You.** There is no going back. If you are gone, you are gone. Life gets hard and problems arise; however, there are amazing moments ahead. Those moments are always worth living for. I am now a presenter for the *National Alliance on Mental Illness* (NAMI). It is an absolute honor to be able to share my story with others in the hope of helping someone else. It is incredible talking to high school students about my journey and hopefully helping them along the way. My most recent co-presenter was remarkable. She spoke with grace and poise about the dark moments in her life. The phrase she ends every presentation with made me

---

42 Melinda Smith, M.A., Lawrence Robinson, and Jeanne Segal, Ph.D., "Depression Symptoms and Warning Signs," Help Guide, last updated September, 2020.

think about my own life. She now is married and has a son. She could not be more thankful for her life.

"There will be moments in your life where amazing things take your breath away, and you'll think to yourself, 'Wow, I'm so glad I'm alive for this.' And those feelings, those moments are worth holding on for."

~JESS HAMMEL [43]

Precious moments are what life is about. Cherish and hold onto the small moments. Staying in the present is something I have started to practice more.

If I would have given up, I would have missed out on so much. I would not have gotten to experience being happy and loving life, getting two kittens, experiencing life with my family, traveling, smiling, laughing, graduating college, driving while blasting music, having many more adventures with my friends, appreciating life, and talking when I need help. There are so many more things I would not have been able to experience had I given up.

The Biggest Blessing from College

Graduating from college was one of my biggest accomplishments. It was the hardest thing I went through. I had many ups and downs, but in the end, it made me much stronger. There were many battles and challenges along the way, but it

---

43   Jess Hamel, *National Alliance on Mental Illness (NAMI) Zoom presentation to Mt. Lebanon High School students, November 30, 2020.*

also gave me the best gift of all: **my best friend from college**. Transferring gave me the most incredible person to share my college experience with. The most beautiful, kind, sweet, caring, loving, and smart person I have ever met. She is my, as we call it, *momma*. She has been there for me through so many hard times and has handled life in the most positive and inspiring way.

This friend has helped me through some of the tough times I experienced and helped me look at my life more positively. It is now my turn to be there for her as she had a mountain thrown at her. She was recently diagnosed with leukemia. No one deserves to ever experience this, especially her. Somehow, some way, she is still so positive and knows she is going to beat it. I keep praying every day. I know she is a fighter and will get through this. A few days after she got her diagnosis, she sent me this beautiful text, and it made me smile knowing she was still being her usual, positive self.

"I have a very good feeling about today! The sun is shining, and I am in very good spirits. I have so many prayers and support and all of my angels in heaven watching over me."

The last time I talked to her on the phone, we joked that she was going to be an author next, and I could for sure see that happening. I know in my heart she will come out on the other side even stronger. I can guarantee she will inspire so many people. She has certainly inspired me by helping me realize life is better when you keep a positive outlook and surround yourself with positive people.

I don't know if she knows how much she has helped and been there for me. She has helped me find the light in so many dark situations. And, after being thrown into such a hard and terrible situation, she knows she can get through it with prayer and positivity. She makes me want to be more positive every day and helps me see the bigger picture. I have no idea who would handle such a life-altering situation in such an inspiring way. She is a magnificent and special person. She makes me see that life is worth fighting for. She is **unbreakable**.

Faith and Grace

Faith is extremely important to me. In fact, faith is how I started to see my life without a dark cloud lingering over my head. Through faith I started to live a more positive and healthy life. My sister has always inspired me with the way she lives her life. She is positive and puts her faith in God. She has helped me see that faith was what I needed to better my life. When I was not relying on God, I was more miserable and depressed. She made me realize I could not live life without having faith in Him. She made me see what I needed to believe. I needed to pray. I needed to trust it would get better.

Whether you believe in God or not, just know there is something to believe in. I lived without trusting in God when I was going down a dark path. Living life with God is so much better for me. He has saved me when I needed Him the most. He will be there for you as well, whether you believe it or not. It is about finding what is right for you. For me, that is, without a doubt, trusting in God with my whole heart and soul. I have never been happier or more content because of Him.

"There is therefore now no condemnation for those who are in Christ Jesus. For the law of the Spirit of life has set you free in Christ Jesus from the law of sin and death."

~ ROMANS 8:1-2 [44]

My freshman year of college I was so depressed I told my family I was not Christian anymore and I did not believe in God. I was so angry with my life that I blamed Him. My family was devastated because they all had a strong faith. There were many times in college where I turned away from my faith. I did not know if it was true or not. I was so upset and at such a low point that I started to wonder if this Christianity thing was fake. I felt free after I gave it all to God. I stopped planning. I stopped worrying as much. I stopped trying to make my life what I "wanted." I had to trust in God's plan.

Please understand I am not telling you to believe one way or another. I am talking about what saved me and set me moving forward. It is, without a doubt, faith. My life has forever changed. I had to understand that I messed up, but that didn't mean I did not deserve God's grace. This is what I believe, but you are entitled to your opinions and beliefs, too.

"Grace, which comes from the Greek New Testament word charis, is God's unmerited favor. It is kindness from God that we don't deserve. There is nothing we have done, nor can ever do to earn this favor. It is a gift from God." [45]

---

44 Romans 8:1-2 (English Standard Version).

45 Mary Fairchild, "What God's Grace Means to Christians: Grace is the Undeserved Love and Favor of God," Learn Religions, Dotdash Publishing, updated June 25, 2019, accessed January 14, 2021.

Prayer became something I did. Praying to feel better was when therapy became a godsend for me. I started taking therapy seriously. My psychiatrist and I changed my medication (there is no shame in taking necessary medication.) Everyone has their own personal beliefs and opinions, but I am talking about what helped me personally. Only you know what will help you. Whatever it may look like to you, believe in it. My life changed when I started to pray for a better life; when I gave my life to God and did not do anything except live. I prayed for peace. I prayed not to be so depressed and not hate life. Let me be clear: my life didn't magically change. God gave me the right tools and people to get to a better and more stable place, and I started to see the light.

A Temporary Problem, A Permanent Decision

It is better to get help and open up than to end your story. There is **nothing** to be ashamed of for feeling the way we sometimes feel. There is help for those times. People who commit suicide leave behind pain, suffering, sadness, despair, emotional trauma, and so many other devastating emotions. Would you ever want to ruin the lives of your parents, family, or friends? I think most of us would say no. Would you want someone to get a phone call telling them the person they love is gone? Or worse, would anyone want to walk in and find someone gone? NO. I wish I was thinking about my loved ones at my times of distress, but of course, mentally I was not thinking straight. What I should have been thinking about when I was at my low point was: *do I really want to hurt the people I love the most by doing something I KNOW I would regret doing?*

Most people who have attempted to kill themselves and failed say they are glad they are still here. Most of them said the second they took pills, jumped, or tried to shoot themselves, they wish they had not. Kevin Hines, who survived jumping from the Golden Gate Bridge, stated that "the moment his fingers left the railing, he felt instant regret."

"I thought it was too late, I said to myself, 'What have I done, I don't want to die,' says Hines, now thirty-eight. 'I realized I made the greatest mistake of my life.'" [46]

When in such a depressive state of mind, it is important to try to look at the good surrounding you. Life sucks sometimes, but it is also beautiful. Life is not ever worth giving up. There is always hope and sometimes you need help to get back on your feet.

Mental health is nothing to joke about, nor should someone be looked down on because of something they are struggling with internally. Mental Health America states:

> *Mental health problems may be related to excessive stress due to a particular situation or series of events. As with cancer, diabetes, and heart disease, mental illnesses are often physical as well as emotional and psychological. Mental illnesses may be caused by a reaction to environmental stresses, genetic factors, biochemical imbalances, or a combination*

---

46 Diane Herbst, "Kevin Hines Survived a Jump Off the Golden Gate Bridge—Now, He's Helping Others Avoid Suicide," *Psycom, Remedy Health Media,* last updated September 9, 2019, accessed January 14, 2021.

of these. With proper care and treatment many individuals learn to cope or recover from a mental illness or emotional disorder. [47]

Depression, anxiety, and mental health conditions should not be faced alone. They are things many people struggle with, but do not talk about, and *that needs to change.*

Purpose

I thought my life was worthless and pointless. I did not matter. No one should ever feel their life is not worth living. That is why talking is so important. Sure, there are always good and bad times, but in the bad times, reach out to someone. This can be someone you deeply trust, such as a doctor. It is better to be safe than sorry. Remember this: no matter what, people are not supposed to fulfill you. It is about fulfilling yourself. That was a hard lesson for me to learn, but it is so true. No one actually "completes" you. You are supposed to complete yourself. There is no person or thing that can sustain your happiness. No boyfriend/girlfriend, game, shoes, or house. You are the only one who can do that. Always remember you are important, and make sure you and your life are being cared for. For me, I let myself discover who I was. What mattered most to me, after I realized its importance, was taking care of myself. I try to help others and be there for them, but I learned I am just as important. I need to make sure I take care of myself before anything else.

---

47 "Mental Illness and the Family: Recognizing Warning Signs and How to Cope," Mental Health America, accessed September 18, 2020.

You do not have to change who you are for anyone. You just need to own who you are. You do not have to change a thing about you. Never let anyone tell you otherwise. These days, I try to look at things in a more positive light. I used to be in a terrible state of mind every day and wondered what my purpose was. I questioned it daily for years. At one point, I thought I did not have a purpose, but I was wrong. Whether someone knows their purpose or not, it is important to remember we all need to be good to each other and help each other along the way. While I have always dreaded having to write for one class assignment or another, I never knew how much writing about things I am passionate about would make me feel so fulfilled. One day it became clear to me that writing was a great way to express my thoughts and emotions because it completely changed how I viewed life. It made me appreciate how the small things are worth savoring. I become more laid back and I was more able to enjoy the journey of life and take a step back to appreciate all the good I have.

I have had quite a long journey up to this point. I know growing up is hard and high school and college are not easy. I know people can be cruel, and feeling excluded sucks, but those are not good people. I have let people make me feel weak, not good enough, worthless, ugly, and stupid. You name it, I have felt it, and you know what? I learned to not let other people define me. It was through hard work in therapy that I was able to move forward and accept my difficult past.

Anyone who makes you feel bad about yourself in any way is not worth it. It is about seeking help and finding the right people, **not** blaming yourself and turning to toxic behavior. The reality is, we all have our struggles and battles, so let's instill more hope in each other. Each person has battles in life.

Find what makes you want to wake up in the morning. I do not mean go find a boyfriend or girlfriend; I mean find your happiness within yourself. If you are in a bad state, trying to add someone else to the mix will only make it worse. It is important to take ownership of your happiness. If you need help finding what makes life worth living, please talk to a doctor. Remember, life **is** worth living. If you have to go to inpatient or outpatient therapy or therapy in general, understand it is not a bad thing. It is there to help you. There is no shame in asking for help. It can build the life you want. You have the power to make life worth living for you and make it even more enjoyable. For years I was belittled and let other people's opinions define me. I wish I had the mindset I have now. If you are in those teen years, please learn from my journey.

Lessons Learned

1. *Find whatever keeps you going and believe in it. It always will get better. Life is worth living.*

Do not just take it from me. Other people who survived suicide attempts state the following:

"We sometimes forget we hurt others in our lives. It causes so much pain and anxiety and fear for our families. We never know what guilt our loved ones are holding on to. It's really not worth it to put family through that loss."

—JESS A. [48]

---

48 Kareem Yasin, "This Is What Suicide Survivors Want You to Know," *Healthline*, updated December 20, 2019.

Life will get better!

"Life can and will get better. You're not alone. There's so many people going through very bad times and people who care about you. Sometimes it seems like a "bad life," but living is worth it. Seek help, find new hobbies, learn to live again, and enjoy little things, cause there's only one opportunity and it is oh so sad to waste it ending this life. Please, don't do it. I promise again, it will get better!"

~MONICA D. [49]

2. Take a Step Back and Check in with Yourself

Think about life in the United Kingdom. There is a certain time everyone stops for tea. Why can't mental health have its own teatime? Why can't we normalize this? It would not be a bad idea to take thirty minutes each day to slow down and mentally check in with ourselves. If we designated a time to give everyone a few minutes to regroup and just have a minute to themselves, who knows how that could help better our own mental health?

3. You Are Never Alone

Seek help if you need it. The second you do not feel okay, talk to someone. There are a lot of people who deal with mental health issues. You are never a burden. You are not a disappointment. You deserve to live a happy, fulfilled life, so let yourself have a second chance. Hope is giving yourself that second chance and believing something is possible.

---

49   Ibid.

4. *Finding the Silver Lining in Your Life*

I do not know what your silver lining is, but I have learned there always is one. Some studies even say that having a journal helps; writing this book is mine. After having a horrible event happen, it changed my perspective on everything. Creating a positive mindset will help you understand that your story is worth living. Studies have shown developing a gratitude journal is a great way to find positives in your own life. Berkley says:

> *Write down up to five things for which you feel grateful. The physical record is important—don't just do this exercise in your head. The things you list can be relatively small in importance (the tasty sandwich I had for lunch today) or relatively large (my sister gave birth to a healthy baby boy). The goal of the exercise is to remember a good event, experience, person, or thing in your life—then enjoy the good emotions that come with it.* [50]

5. *You Are Here for a Reason. There Is a Purpose for You.*

This is easier said than done for someone in a frantic state of mind; however, the second your mind goes to these thoughts, it is important to address them immediately. If you give yourself a chance, you can live a happy and positive life. Hitting rock bottom does not mean you need to stay there. You can change it. You have the power to make a difference in your life. Please do what you need to. You deserve the chance

---

50 "Gratitude Journal (Greater Good in Action)," *Greater Good in Action-Science-based Practices for a Meaningful Life,* University of California Berkeley, accessed September 29, 2020.

to find your happiness, no matter what that is. Even going outside for a simple walk helps. Do what you can to make the changes you need to be a better you.

What is something you can do that will make you feel fulfilled?

CHAPTER 6

Addressing the Stigma

Empathy: The action of understanding, being aware of, being sensitive to, and vicariously experiencing the feelings, thoughts, and experience of another of either the past or present without having the feelings, thoughts, and experience fully communicated in an objectively explicit manner. [51]

One of the biggest issues we have today is silence. We choose not to talk about the issues going on in the world. Instead, we have become so consumed with the media and social media that we act like certain issues do not need to be talked about. We ignore them. We are not saying anything when we should be saying something. We need to use our voices to end anyone feeling "less than" for their feelings.

When you're driving, have you ever thought about where the other drivers are going? You have no idea where they're headed or if they are in a rush. You have no idea where they are coming from. Think about it: you do not know their story. You only know what you see when they drive

---

51   Merriam-Webster, s.v. "empathy (n.)," accessed October 1, 2020

past you. That is how we seem to act around our own lives. No one knows what you are going through and you don't know what someone else is dealing with. Someone who lashed out might have gotten fired or received the news that they have a serious health condition. If we tried to empathize with each other more, we might find ourselves in a better place. This mindset could help end the stigma around mental illness.

In talking with a local psychologist, I found out some interesting information about what typically happens with younger clients. It does not matter if it is a boy or a girl— talking about your feelings is helpful. She said that therapy is not only useful when you are depressed and upset, but it is helpful to utilize and take seriously all the time. She also explained that going to a few therapists helps you find the right one for you. You never know if someone is the right fit until you give it a full chance. I think if people did this, we would be living in a healthier world. If you tried it and it does not work for you, that's okay, but you may not have found the right one. She told me that "my client is twenty years old and his mother reached out to me. He wasn't suicidal, but he was down and depressed." Therapy is not only useful when in a crisis, but also when going to it regularly in order to build coping skills to help when a crisis occurs.

Giving myself a chance to find the right psychologist/psychiatrist took time. It took seeing a few different people until I found someone with whom I connected and felt comfortable opening up to. I was not emotionally opening up for the longest time. As a result, I was not getting the most out of therapy because it terrified me; however, the longer I would go to someone, much like any relationship, I became more comfortable and at ease. I often arrived late for a session or canceled "with a good reason." Those reasons often included tests, overload of homework, or sleep. It got so bad that my therapist told my mother she did not think she could help me since I was not taking it seriously. This conversation was a wake-up call for me. The second I was responsible and went consistently, it helped me. I saw how much I screwed myself over by not putting my all into it. I did not want to admit how much I could have previously benefited if only I would have taken it seriously earlier.

Therapy can be a super rewarding way to sift through the emotional baggage that's holding you back. But because it involves being vulnerable and diving into some pretty murky subjects and feelings, you might find yourself indulging in self-sabotaging behaviors that halt your progress—and you may not even realize it. Therapists call these therapy-interfering behaviors (TIBs), and the fascinating thing about them is most of us don't realize when or why we're getting in our own way. "We're quick to make excuses, and slow to recognize patterns of behavior in ourselves," said California-based licensed psychologist Caroline Fleck. These behaviors function to protect us from feeling or thinking painful things in the context of therapy, yet paradoxically, interfere with our emotional growth. [52]

52   Krissy Brady, "13 Signs You Are Sabotaging Your Own Progress in Therapy: Therapists Reveal How to Know If You Aren't Getting the Most Out of Your Therapy Sessions and How to Fix It," *Huffpost*, September 19, 2019.

One Step at a Time

Anxiety has always affected me daily. I would get anxious about everything. I'd get stomach pains that made me feel sick. As I got older, the more I realized the many great benefits that come from attending therapy sessions regularly. Anxiety is hard to deal with alone. Being able to talk about these feelings and emotions to someone else in a safe environment is beneficial.

> One of the fastest ways to erase the stigma associated with counseling is to realize that you are not alone. Because many people are hesitant to discuss their struggles, you may not realize just how common it is to seek some form of professional help, whether it is to work on an intimate relationship or process through a childhood trauma. According to a survey by the American Counseling Association released in 2011, anxiety disorders affected forty million Americans ages eighteen and older in 2009 (about 18 percent of the demographic). However, anxiety is not the only common struggle. The American Mental Health Counselors Association reported that in a given year, 20 percent of the population experiences a mental disorder. [53]

Taking a major step in making a huge change and turning another direction is sometimes the only solution to getting long-lasting results. During my sophomore year in college, I still was not doing too well mentally. I was living at home, which was better, but I still constantly felt that my life was

---

53   "How to Overcome the Cultural Stigma Surrounding Counseling," Bradley University, accessed January 14, 2021.

about to burst into flames. This feeling kept me depressed. I was still doing therapy with a psychologist every week, but it was not doing much for me because I was not letting her in. Instead, I shut myself down and did not mention everything going on. On the few occasions where I did happen to speak up, I did not feel any better. I felt misunderstood and no one knew where I was coming from. My therapist introduced me to DPT, which is Dialectic Behavior Therapy. She would give me worksheets and papers all the time, but I would just get rid of them. I thought everything was bullshit and continued down my dark path.

"*Dialectical behavioral therapy (DBT) is a type of cognitive behavioral therapy. Cognitive behavioral therapy tries to identify and change negative thinking patterns and pushes for positive behavioral changes.*" [54]

Since I did not do the work when given the worksheets, I did not make any progress. I wish I would have taken advantage of the resources and tools I had access to because then another storm happened, and I did not have the coping skills in place to deal with it. I had not yet dealt with all of my inner demons. I may have looked better from the outside, but I was definitely not okay.

I had a friend who was living at home, too. She started to see that I was in a bad place. I would tell her all the time, "I am going to kill myself. I can't" and "I can't do this anymore." These statements obviously alarmed her, and when I changed

---

54 Reviewed by Smitha Bhandari, MD, "Dialectical Behavioral Therapy," *WebMD*, February 18, 2020, accessed January 14, 2021.

clothes, she would see the harm I had done to myself. She was a good friend and told her dad that I needed **serious** help. Her dad talked to mine soon after she told him what was going on. A few days later, my parents came to talk to me again. They handed me a sheet of paper which read *Intensive Outpatient Therapy*. It was a three day a week, three hours a day program that did not involve a hospital stay. The one recommended to us was for college-aged students. I read the sheet of paper and freaked out. I asked them why all of this was happening. They explained how my friend was so worried and scared for my life that she told her dad, which upset me. My parents also told me that the therapist I was seeing had recommended this program for me, which is when they knew my depression was getting worse and not better. Something had to change.

Telling someone they need help are words no one wants to hear. In fact, I went through a few different stages with this. First came denial, anger, resentment, and then acceptance. Not everyone responds in this manner, but I refused to admit I actually needed to get help. I believed I only harmed once in a while, when I felt I deserved it. It is not like I did it every day, I was "fine." Meanwhile, I was actually a mess. Once my parents told me I had to go to this program, I immediately blew up and refused. They told me I was the one who had to decide, and they could not force me. I was relieved for a moment. A few weeks later I thought about ending my life again. I thought transferring schools would have made things better, not worse. I was losing hope again. I thought maybe I should be done until I remembered the paper my parents gave me. I called the number and scheduled an evaluation. After my evaluation, they told me I needed their program. That was terrifying, I had no idea what I was in for.

Intensive Treatment Is a Go

Feeling crazy, judged, and useless were feelings I had felt every day for years. I felt there was something seriously wrong with me. Outpatient therapy with other people who wanted to die was excruciating and draining. We all were struggling deeply; outpatient therapy is not fun. It is what it sounds like: intense and miserable. Miserable because three nights a week for hours I would be in group therapy with people who had the same issues I did. The first day I walked in, there was a table and other people around it. I was so scared. I just wanted to be better. I just wanted to be okay. I knew this was going to be draining and I had to answer some incredibly difficult questions. I was handed a piece of paper which had one statement.

I am alive because...

Chills rushed through my entire body because the first thing I could think of was my family. At this point, I knew I was alive for a reason—for them. I needed to stay alive for them and anyone else who was close to me, but more importantly, for **myself**. I stared at the sheet of paper for a minute and started crying. I thought so much about my family and realized I could not do that to them or my friends. I had to somehow get a better mindset because they did not deserve to deal with the pain I could cause. I knew at that moment I was exactly where I needed to be.

> An **intensive outpatient program** *(IOP) is a kind of treatment service and support program used predominantly to treat eating disorders, bipolar disorder (including mania; and for types I and II), unipolar depression, self-harm, and chemical dependency.*

> *IOP's often operate on a small scale and do not require the rig-*
> *orous residential or partial day services typically offered by the*
> *larger, more comprehensive treatment facilities.* [55]

As incredibly hard as it was to admit I needed help, it was one of the best things I have ever done for myself. It gave me a chance to open up and figure out the root of my issues. On top of that, while in outpatient I met with a psychiatrist who prescribed different medication for me, helping me get stable. Needing help does not need to be frowned upon. Plenty of people have sought out treatment. It can be used for all different types of mental illness. This is something everyone needs to be aware is an option if needed. Get the help that will better your life. The stigma is nothing. Your mental health is everything.

Everyone Is Struggling

No matter what, you are not alone. It does not matter who you are; we all have battles on this journey called life. We have different issues and situations being thrown our way. We have to learn how to cope with life in a positive manner. We have to remember that both men and women are facing mental health issues. Men struggle and have feelings, too. One of my guy friends recently shared with me his struggles with mental health issues and how it had affected him personally.

> *"Men are supposed to be strong and not have feelings, but that's not the case at all. We're all human. We all go through things and experience different feelings that sometimes we need help dealing with."*

---

55 "Are Intensive Outpatient Treatment Programs the Future of Mental Health?" Botkiss Center for Recovery, August 28, 2019, accessed January 15, 2021.

Since he was someone who had done inpatient therapy, he gained a new perspective by being placed in a diverse group of people with different ages and problems. He said that by doing inpatient, he gained a new perspective of what he had to be thankful for.

"I didn't really understand myself or the feelings at the time. I was forced to take medication and go to therapy that I didn't really understand, and I felt didn't really help. It took me growing up a lot to realize what was going on."

As he got older, he learned how to deal with his feelings and thoughts. He said getting through suicidal moments requires talking and focusing on moving forward, because there is not much you can do when someone is in that state of mind. He brought up the stigma surrounding mental health and how people treat you differently if they think you are crazy and cannot handle yourself. It is okay to have help and get advice.

"The only way to get better is to move forward one step at a time and learn from your mistakes. Constantly looking back at your mistakes doesn't help."

Lessons Learned

1. *Therapy Doesn't Make You Weak*

Having therapy regularly has helped me immensely. I recommend it for anyone needing help. Sometimes we need to take a step back, reevaluate, and vent without hearing a ton of differing opinions. In every single environment, you deserve to feel comfortable and free from hostility and judgment from others. Let's start to better everyone's mental health by being open and kind to each other. We can all learn something from each other regardless of our age groups because we all have something unique to bring to the world.

2. Outpatient or Inpatient Treatment Is Normal

While doing outpatient therapy was exhausting, it was also rewarding for my future self. Looking back, I see it was exactly what I needed, even though it required a lot of time. I was in a place where I needed significant help, which is why I did the intensive-outpatient therapy program.

3. Don't Let Others Deter You from Getting What You Need

The stigma around mental health was in my head for the longest time until I realized it did not matter what anyone else had to say. All that mattered was I was getting the proper care that I needed. Men, women, it does not matter—everyone deserves access to treatment without judgment.

4. True Friendship

I was angry when my friend went to her father about me. What I did not realize at the time was that she was doing it because she was frightened and wanted me to get better. It was not malicious. When in that state, it is not uncommon to push someone away who is trying to help you. In the end, because she did not keep it to herself, I was given the opportunity to develop better coping skills.

Just like with many difficult subjects in life, people feel fearful and uncertain of how to respond when they suspect a loved one is self-harming. Will I make it worse if I call attention to it? Will they get mad at me? What do I say? Maybe it is just a phase and it will go away? But, just as with other difficult life events, acknowledging the issue is a caring and supportive act. When we don't ask if someone is hurting, they often feel more isolated, alone, and invisible. [56]

5. Many Treatment Options Are Available

Seeking help when you need it is okay. It is also okay to get different types of mental health treatment, because you may need different types of care at specific times in your life. Stop suffering in silence. Not enough people are reaching out to take care of their mental health.

Unfortunately, only about 41 percent of adults in the US with a mental health condition received mental health services in 2017. Among adults with a serious mental illness, 62.9 percent received mental health services in the past year. Furthermore, serious mental illness costs America $193.2 billion in lost earnings per year. So many individuals do not get the care that they need. IOPs [Intensive Outpatient Programs] could help close this gap. [57]

How can we be the change that ends the stigma?

---

56 Katherine DeVries, "Tips for Talking to Someone About Self-Harm," Pine Rest Christian Mental Health Services, accessed February 1, 2021.

57 "Are Intensive Outpatient Treatment Programs the Future of Mental Health?" Botkiss Center for Recovery, August 28, 2019, accessed January 15, 2021.

CHAPTER 7

Overcoming Disturbance

———

Self-harm: The practice of deliberately injuring yourself, for example by cutting yourself, as a result of having serious emotional or mental problems. [58]

Mental health is how people think about things, respond to events in their lives, and treat themselves. I know when you are feeling down and depressed each person has a certain way of coping. Sometimes that coping mechanism may be toxic and destructive. Recognizing that a coping mechanism is harmful is a step toward making healthy changes. Believe you can make positive changes. I know you can.

Disclaimer: Please never self-harm. It is *not* a healthy way of coping. There are so many other ways to cope with life's struggles in a healthy manner. Seeking out help is the answer.

---

58 *Oxford Learner's Dictionary, s.v.* "self-harm (n.)," accessed February 1, 2021.

If you have ever self-harmed in the past, do not be ashamed. Let it be a part of your past not your present or future.

We need to do more with our lives besides just surviving. We can make positive changes for ourselves if we **allow** it. Whether it is self-harm or something else negatively impacting our mental health, it is important to recognize what we are doing and change it. Through helping ourselves and being open about it, we can allow our stories to help others. Sharing our stories and not being ashamed is so important. Seeking help to identify and develop healthy coping skills can create positive changes in your life. Getting help can allow you to put negative actions in the past. We all have cycles to break simply because no one is perfect.

> *The risk of NSSI (Non-Suicidal Self-Injury) is particularly high in adolescence; the mean age at onset peaks around the age of fourteen to fifteen. A second peak is common around the age of twenty in college samples. Self-injury is often episodic, which means people will use it for a while but may go days, months, or even years without self-injury episodes or urges before self-injuring again.* [59]

My Disturbing Reality

Tori DeAngelis references *The Journal of American College Health* in an article she wrote for the American Psychological Association:

---

59   Janis Whitlock, Stephen P. Lewis, Imke Baetens, and Penelope Hasking, "Non-Suicidal Self-Injury on College Campuses," *Higher Education Today (blog)*, American Council on Higher Education, February 6, 2019.

The most frequent sites of self-injury are the hands, wrists, stomach, and thighs, though self-injurers may hurt themselves anywhere on the body. Results can be serious: about a third of students reporting NSSI (Non-Suicidal Self-Injury) in two college studies said they had hurt themselves so badly that they should have been seen by a medical professional, but only 5 percent sought treatment, according to a random sample of students in eight colleges and universities reported in a 2011 article by Whitlock and colleagues in the Journal of American College Health. [60]

Even before I went to boarding school, I had a friend my freshmen year of high school who was as mentally unstable as I was. We hung out a lot and became practically inseparable. One day I was at her house talking as we usually did, and I noticed something visible on her body that concerned me. I knew something was up, and I had a good idea of what was going on.

I said to her sternly, "What the hell is that?"

"What? Nothing," she responded.

I knew it was not nothing, so I said again, "What is that?"

"What is what?" She tried to be coy.

"Is that what I think it is?"

---

60 Tori DeAngelis, "Who Self-Injures," American Psychological Association, July/August 2015, Vol 46, no. 7.

"Oh, that. Yeah, sometimes I cut to feel better. You should try it. It helps."

I could not believe what I was hearing. I thought it absolutely insane that someone could harm themselves and not understand how wrong it was. If only I would have known then that the words, *"You should try it, it helps"* would lead to a treacherous and destructive path for me months later. I might have been able to save myself a lot of trouble. As hard as this is to write today, my self-harming began when I was a sophomore in high school, and it went on for years. Researchers from Cornell and Princeton studied how prevalent self-harm is among college students.

> *About 17 percent of college students—20 percent of women and 14 percent of men—report that they have cut, burned, carved, or harmed themselves in other ways, reports a new survey by Cornell and Princeton University researchers, the largest study on self-injurious behavior (SIB) in the United States to date. However, fewer than 7 percent of the students studied had ever sought medical help for their self-inflicted physical injuries.* [61]

The Scary Truth

The reality is more people are struggling with self-harm than most would think. This is a widespread, serious issue that needs to be addressed by society. Serious help, not judgment, is what is needed. *The Recovery Village* webpage sites a study

---

61 Susan S. Lang, "Self-Injury is Prevalent Among College Students, but Few Seek Medical Help, Study by Cornell and Princeton Researchers Finds," *Cornell Chronicle*, June 5, 2006.

from across 40 countries. This study found that about 17 percent of people will end up hurting themselves in their lifetime. This is a staggering statistic. The realization that the average age when self-harming starts is thirteen made my jaw drop. I could not believe what I was reading. Thirteen years old is the **average** age for starting to self-harm. That means that there are kids younger than thirteen doing it. Every kid needs a chance to live their adolescent lives without inflicting themselves pain. [62]

There is another shocking statistic in *The Recovery Village* webpage: 45 percent of people use cutting as their method of self-injury. That means 55 percent are using another method. For me, binge drinking became my other method of self-harm as I tried to dull my pain. Of the people who want to get help, about half will talk to their friends rather than professionals. Talking to friends can be a good start, but most people do not know how to effectively help someone who self-injures. Many people are struggling, and *no one* deserves that. [63]

People are not always aware of what is being done in secret. It is important to check-in with your loved ones regularly because people who seem "fine" may in fact not be "fine." When I was in that state of depression, my thoughts were not about if self-harming was right or wrong. I felt I deserved to feel the pain. I felt I deserved it because of how depressed and miserable I was. I would let my terrible state of mind take over because I was at such a low point in my life. I tried to

---

62   Megan Hull, editor, "Self-Harm Statistics and Facts," The Recovery Village, updated December 23, 2020, accessed January 17, 2021.

63   Ibid.

keep it a secret for as long as I could until I finally received intense help. Raising awareness about how common self-harm is helps victims get the right support and helps their friends and family spot warning signs.

Healthy Ways to Cope with Life

Learning alternatives can help move someone away from self-destructive behavior to more healthy and positive ways of coping. By learning healthy coping skills, I did myself a favor. Even using a fidget spinner or stress ball to handle situations is a more effective and healthy way of dealing with stress and diminishing the desire to self-harm or binge drink. Having a plan set in place for when impulsive feelings happen is helpful. It can be calling a friend, going for a run, or some other sort of physical activity to get endorphins up that can rid impulsive feelings.

You Got This

No one can get better for you. You have to break the cycle yourself. You have to decide to live because no one can live for you. You can become anything you want, but only if you give yourself the chance to develop healthier ways to cope. You have to be the one who fights to get better and believes there is much more to life. I have been there. I know how hard it is. I was down so deep wanting nothing more than to just end it all, but I came out on the other side. I felt completely done and defeated until the day I decided to change.

It hit me pretty quickly that I needed to get my life together after one final episode where, once again, my sister helped me turn my life around. I was tired of always feeling sad and on edge. I knew there had to be a better way and started to take my therapy seriously.

Believe me, if you start trying to cope more positively right now, you will see a change in your life, because I sure did. A better way to cope can include something called Positive Reframing.

In general, healthy coping mechanisms are those strategies that help you deal with stress, illness, or trauma effectively with no harmful consequences. Many of them are evidence-based strategies, and some of them are learned through experiences or others' experiences as well.

Some examples of healthy coping mechanisms include the following:

Positive Reframing: *Simply put, positive reframing is the ability to see the bright side of any given situation. A study published in The Royal Society claims that focusing on positive emotions "spark" actions that help people rise above their situation. For example, coping with addiction in the family can be difficult—but when accompanied by positive emotions such as hope, it is followed by an action such as deciding to go to rehab.*

Finding Support: *Another effective way of coping with problems is through seeking support. Support can be found in the form of expert help or peers who are going through the same struggles. For example, people who are coping with addiction and PTSD can seek support in dual diagnosis centers along* *with talk therapy groups for those who have substance use and PTSD.*

Relaxation: People dealing with anxiety can use relaxation techniques as a means to cope. Deep breathing, meditation, or nature therapy are all strategies that promote relaxation. [64]

Lessons Learned

1. Say Something if Struggling Silently

Say something and get help, because denial is even more destructive and causes more issues.

There were three main things I did differently after receiving treatment:

- Learned to cope in effective, healthy ways.
- Learned to take care of myself which means it is okay to be "selfish" and stop worrying about what everyone else thought of me.
- Became more confident in who I was and learned to love myself (though I still have my days just like anyone else).

2. Always Check in with Your Loved Ones

It might not be a comfortable conversation to have with someone you deeply care for, but it's helpful to listen and

---

64 "Coping Strategies & Addiction: Recovery Skills and Tools for Coping," Sunshine Behavioral Health, accessed October 15, 2020.

encourage the person to get help. The National Alliance on Mental Illness states:

"Gently encourage someone to get treatment by stating that self-harm isn't uncommon and doctors and therapists can help. If possible, offer to help find treatment. But don't go on the offensive and don't try to make the person promise to stop, as it takes more than willpower to quit." [65]

3. Staying Active Helps

Healthline states the following about physical activity:

Endorphins are only one of many neurotransmitters released when you exercise. Physical activity also stimulates the release of dopamine, norepinephrine, and serotonin. These brain chemicals play an important part in regulating your mood. For example, regular exercise can positively impact serotonin levels in your brain. Raising your levels of serotonin boosts your mood and overall sense of well-being. It can also help improve your appetite and sleep cycles, which are often negatively affected by depression. Regular exercise also helps balance your body's level of stress hormones, such as adrenaline. Adrenaline plays a crucial role in your fight-or-flight response, but too much of it can damage your health. [66]

---

65 "Self-Harm," National Alliance on Mental Illness, accessed October 16, 2020.

66 Ryan Collins, "Exercise, Depression, and the Brain," *Healthline*, Healthline Media, July 25, 2017.

4. Take Action in the Best Way Possible

The more people told me I needed to cope differently and live life differently pushed me to do the opposite. Based on my experience, do not try and help a person directly because they will deny they are doing anything harmful. Talk to someone you trust, whether that is their parent, doctor, sibling, etc.

5. Don't Be Ashamed If You Have Scars

Opening up about harming yourself in the past or present can be intimidating. Asking for help or telling your story is nothing to be ashamed of. If you have ever harmed yourself in the past, understand you are not crazy or fucked up. I used to think I was both of those things when, in reality, I just needed help. I realize now it is not the right way to handle life and it can break your loved ones' hearts. I am happy to say that even though I have scars, I am past it now that I have learned of other ways to cope. Some of the best ways are working out, staying active, and practicing mindfulness.

There is nothing to be ashamed of if you need help.

Check in with yourself.

Should you seek help? If so, please see the following resources:

Resources

In the US–Call the National Suicide Prevention Lifeline at 1-800-273-TALK (8255) or IMAlive at 1-800-784-2433.

The Trevor Project offers suicide prevention services for LGBTQ youth at **1-866-488-7386.**

SAMHSA's National Helpline offers referrals for substance abuse and mental health treatment at **1-800-662-4357.**

In the UK and Ireland–Call Samaritans UK at 116 123

In Australia–Call Lifeline Australia at 13 11 14

In other countries–Visit IASP or Suicide.org to find a helpline in your country. [67]

---

67 Jaelline Jaffe, Ph.D., Lawrence Robinson, and Jeanne Segal, Ph.D., "Are You Feeling Suicidal?" HelpGuide.org, last updated September 2020, accessed September 13, 2020.

PART 3

CHAPTER 8

But I Want to Live

———

Consequence: A result or effect of an action or condition. [68]

Every decision we make, every interaction we have—every-thing incurs consequences. Each choice you make can have an impact on your life. Your choices are either good or bad. The choice to change your life can be unsettling, so knowing your actions can affect not just you but also people around you carries a lot of weight. A decision can have either good or bad consequences. It is vitally important to realize this so you can make wise choices to live life to its full potential.

Living life and not worrying about every little thing is important. In reality, however, it is also important to be smart and control what we can control. No matter what we do, there are going to be repercussions for our actions. The only difference is whether they are good or bad. Deciding to do something you think is good may backfire or create a great outcome. Our actions and our words can affect someone else, so we need to acknowledge it. We

---

68   *Oxford English Dictionary, s.v.* "Consequence (n.)," accessed January 24, 2021.

sometimes do not know what the consequence of our actions are, yet we also know if we choose wisely, it will most likely give us a better result; unfortunately, we are impatient and want to see the consequences immediately. That rarely happens.

> *The connection between action and outcome is not always a linear one, according to Tina Grotzer at the Harvard Graduate School of Education. Take pollution: "If you dump oil or garbage down the drain in Cambridge, you have no way of knowing that it is actually affecting the water in Boston Harbor. You don't make the connection, because you can't see the outcome," says Grotzer. Consequences don't always follow a directly observable pathway.* [69]

By making smart choices, the results usually work out in the end. When we make bad choices, we know we are most likely going to have a problem. Take drunk driving. If someone is drunk and decides to drive a car, their action risks not just their life, but anyone else in their car, in the cars around them, as well as the pedestrians they pass. Driving drunk can never be tolerated. Drunk driving kills people. The consequences are never good. On the other hand, the consequence of having a designated driver or calling an Uber gives people a chance to get home safely and not put themselves and so many others at risk.

---

69   Ruth E. C. Prince, "Connections, Consequences and Understanding: Encouraging Teachers and Students to Approach Science from a Broader Perspective," *Usable Knowledge,* Harvard Graduate School of Education, May 29, 2008.

In 2017 there were 10,874 people killed in alcohol-impaired driving crashes, an average of one alcohol-impaired driving fatality every forty-eight minutes. These alcohol-impaired-driving fatalities accounted for 29 percent of all motor vehicle traffic fatalities in the United States in 2017. Of the 10,874 people who died in alcohol-impaired driving crashes in 2017, there were 6,618 drivers (61 percent) who had BACs (Blood Alcohol Content) of .08 g/dL or higher. The remaining fatalities consisted of 3,075 motor vehicle occupants (28%) and 1,181 nonoccupants (11%). [70]

Smart Decisions, Smart Outcomes

Consequences are not always negative. Some actions are going to create good consequences. For example, think of therapy. Going to therapy and being vulnerable with your therapist will give you the consequence of making potential discoveries about yourself, healing areas of hurt, and helping you feel better. It is incredibly rewarding. I had the pleasure of speaking with Michelle Decker of the National Alliance of Mental Illness (NAMI). She is now a Young Adult Outreach and Education Specialist. Mental health is important to Michelle because she was in a bad place during college. Instead of overdosing, which would have had a horrible consequence, she chose to check herself into inpatient therapy. She made the choice to call for help. She would never be where she is today had she not made that one call.

---

70 National Highway Traffic Safety Administration, "Alcohol Impaired Driving," November, 2018, accessed February 2, 2021

"I knew I needed help, so I called 911 myself and checked myself into inpatient therapy."

~MICHELLE DECKER

Today, Michelle is deeply involved in mental health advocacy and a presenter for NAMI. She has shared her story hoping to help others with their own journey. She recognizes the consequence that, by being vulnerable, she actually helps people, and that gives her joy. She went from being in a bad place in her life where she wanted to give up to now helping people not feel inadequate and understand it is okay to reach out. This is a wonderful consequence. She is very happy with where she is in life today. She is strong and an example of why being vulnerable can lead to a great consequence: happiness.

Seat Belt NOW!

March 14, 2020 was the last day bars were open before COVID-19 shut everything down, and everyone went into quarantine in my town. I was invited to a party that night and told to bring some of my friends. Only one of my friends went because no one else wanted to go. She did not stay at the party for long, and after she left, the guy who invited me, some of his friends and I went to another party and then to hang out at their apartment. The designated driver was sober. I climbed into the middle of the back seat between the guy I liked and his friend. It did not dawn on me that I did not have my seat belt on. We were driving down a four-lane road with lots of side streets with stop signs for vehicles coming out onto the main road. I was talking to one of the guys when I realized I didn't have my seat belt on. As I secured it, we saw a car flying down a side street toward us, not stopping at the stop sign.

We all screamed.

I thought this was going to be the end of us. Like a horrific flash in a movie of a car accident scene, we were T-boned. The only thing I knew after the impact and when the car stopped moving was that I was still alive. I did not know what had happened. Thankfully, I had put my seat belt on just in time. A few seconds after the crash, I unbuckled myself. Everyone had gotten out of the car and made it to the sidewalk before me. One of the guys was *covered* in blood. I did not know what to do. I was scared and in shock. I sat down next to him and put his head in my lap so he didn't hit his head on the ground. I screamed, asking if everyone was alive. To my extreme relief, everyone answered. I called 911 since I had my phone in my hand.

"Every day in America, another twenty-nine people die as a result of drunk driving crashes. That's one person every fifty minutes." [71]

Both cars were totaled. The driver that hit us backed up his car and parked it on the other side of the street. He then got out of the car, abandoned it, and ran. He disappeared. I was angry beyond belief. My whole body shook and throbbed. We could have been dead for all he knew. Several police cars and three ambulances got to the scene and immediately

---

71 MADD, "Statistics: Fight Back against Misinformation. Get the Facts," accessed January 24, 2021.

blocked off the street. They tried to get as much detail about the accident as possible, but the other driver was nowhere to be found. All of us were taken to the hospital.

Post-Traumatic Stress Disorder (PTSD)

Once I got to the emergency room, I was in a hospital bed alone and afraid. I did the only thing I knew how to: I prayed. I prayed I did not have a brain bleed due to hitting my head; the doctors wanted to check right away. After being alone for thirty minutes (it was around 1:30 a.m.), my mom arrived. I was in shock. We both prayed I would be okay and hoped my head injury was not serious. I was eventually diagnosed with a concussion, among other injuries. Many tests later (around 5:00 a.m.), I was released to go home. I was beyond terrified when I got into my mom's car. I wanted to go home but I was shaking.

Post-Traumatic Stress Disorder is a real thing.

One serious psychological consequence often associated with serious MVAs (Motor Vehicle Accidents) is post-traumatic stress disorder (PTSD). PTSD is an anxiety disorder that often follows a traumatic event involving actual or threatened death, serious injury, or threat to the physical integrity of oneself or others (American Psychiatric Association, 2000.) For many individuals, the symptoms of PTSD following a serious MVA may include psychologically re-experiencing the trauma (e.g., intrusive thoughts about the accident, distressing dreams about the accident), persistent avoidance of thoughts or situations associated with the accident (e.g., reluctance or refusal to drive, actively avoiding thoughts about the MVA), numbing of emotional responsiveness (e.g., greatly reduced or absence of emotions, feeling detached from others), and increased physical arousal (e.g., exaggerated startle, irritability, disturbed sleep). [72]

Driving home with my mom was terrifying even though it was early morning with no traffic. In the following days, I did not want to get into a car, let alone drive. At my appointment with my neuropsychologist for my concussion (my mother had driven me there), he told me I needed to get back behind the wheel and start driving again. It was hard and continues to be to this day. If a car approaches from a side street or on-ramp, I am overly aware and cautious; this happens whether I am driving or a passenger. I have talked to my therapist about it, and time and many more miles in a car have helped me not have as many flashbacks.

Lessons Learned

1. People Suffer Based on Poor Choices of Others

Making poor choices results in some serious consequences not only for yourself but for those around you.

"It is normal for adolescents to have a sense of being uniquely invincible, to have an 'it will never happen to me' mindset. This way of thinking may limit their ability to assess situations,

---

72 J. Gayle Beck and Scott F. Coffey, "Assessment and Treatment of PTSD After a Motor Vehicle Collision: Empirical Findings and Clinical Observations," US National Library of Medicine, National Center for Biotechnology Information, May 28, 2008.

risks, and future consequences. As a result, they may engage in risky behaviors and test authority." [73]

2. Do Not Drive Drunk

It is never worth it to put your own life, as well as so many others, at risk based on this poor decision. We were extremely lucky to be alive after our accident. So many of us had injuries, but we should not have had to deal with them in the first place. We have to deal with them because of another person's **BAD** decision.

3. Never Get in the Car of Someone Who Is Driving under the Influence

The guy driving the car in my accident was **not** drunk. He was a victim of someone else choosing to drive recklessly. Having no control of the outcome of an accident caused by someone else is the absolute worst feeling in the world.

4. WEAR A SEAT BELT!

My intuition or gut feeling knew something treacherous was about to happen. I do believe God spoke to me and said, "Put your seat belt on, now!" I believe it saved my life. Who knows, if I had not done that, I could have been even more seriously injured or gone through the windshield and died. God saved me.

---

73   Susan C. Kim, M.D., Kathleen Romito, M.D. and John Pope, M.D., "How Adolescent Thinking Develops," University of Michigan Health System, Healthwise, Inc., August 21, 2019, accessed February 2, 2021.

5. Find the Silver Lining in a Terrible Situation

I did not get overwhelmed by anger, even when police did not find the other driver. I channeled my emotions into something positive. That is how this book began. After the accident, I started thinking about the number two. I had no idea why until one day, while recovering on the couch, I realized I had faced death twice. One almost happened by my choice, and the other was caused by someone else. I prayed and thanked God for keeping me alive both times because I did not want to die. I wanted to live because something in me knew I had so much more to live for. I had to see it for myself.

Drunk driving is not worth it!

Will you make sure you have your seatbelt on?

CHAPTER 9

Don't Look Back

———

Regret: Sorrow aroused by circumstances beyond one's control or power to repair.[74]

Part of life is learning through the different experiences we face. We have the power to take our past experiences and turn them into something useful. Our past experiences should be used as a good teacher to better our lives in the future. We all learn through trial and error. Nothing in life is perfect. Sometimes we say or do the wrong thing because we are all human, and sometimes we get it right.

It's often easy to get mad at ourselves and feel guilt when we do something we wish we had not. We then feel regret. We are all human and make mistakes. We all get ourselves into wrong situations. Of course, there are things we wish we did not do; nonetheless, it is a valuable lesson to continue to move forward in a positive manner and learn from those situations. We learn more each day. Kathryn Schulz, a staff writer for *The New Yorker*, discusses in a TED Talk the most

———

74   Merriam-Webster, s.v., "Regret (n.)," accessed October 14, 2020.

common regrets we experience in life and how we seem to ponder our decisions and wish we chose a different outcome. However, we cannot go back and dwell incessantly on what we did wrong.

> *The things we regret most in life: number one by far, education. Thirty-three percent of our regrets pertain to decisions we made about education. We wish we'd gotten more of it. We wish we'd taken better advantage of the education that we did have. We wish we'd chosen to study a different topic. Others very high on our list of regrets include career, romance, parenting, various decisions and choices about our sense of self and how we spend our leisure time, or actually more specifically, how we fail to spend our leisure time. The remaining regrets pertain to these things: finance, family issues unrelated to romance or parenting, health, friends, spirituality, and community.* [75]

I have been in plenty of situations I've immediately regretted. I would beat myself up for saying or doing the wrong thing, which would ultimately lead to serious self-depreciation. Beating yourself up, regretting past decisions, and not moving past them will only affect your mental health. I have to remind myself often to learn from those mistakes and move on. Life will work out the way it is supposed to. There is no point for me to wallow in regret for what has happened in my past, because I can't do anything about it now. I can only learn and move on. What's done is done.

---

75   Kathryn Schulz, "Don't Regret Regret," filmed November 2011 at Ted-Studios, New York, NY, video, 16:36.

A Blessing in Disguise

When I started my freshman year at college, within weeks I knew I had made one of the worst decisions of my life. Because of that decision, I have learned so much about myself and figured out who I am by going through that hardship. I would never want anyone else to face the struggles I encountered. I believe I went through it so I could help someone else not go through what I did. I hope others see that even through the rough times, life is a journey. It is never worth giving up. My freshman year was an obstacle given to me that I had to overcome. Through it, I became even stronger and more able to fight for the most precious gift of all—life. If I would have chosen a different college, I never would have met someone who encouraged me and persuaded me to follow through with writing a book. She believed in me. She knew I had a story and a voice that needed to be heard.

I look at those times as a learning and growing experience instead of regretting the past. Giving yourself the benefit of the doubt and letting yourself make mistakes is a part of life. We should not let ourselves get stuck in our past regrets. Forgive yourself and learn valuable lessons that can help better your future.

> "We all have regrets about decisions we make that didn't go according to plan," said Laura Reagan, LCSW-C, an integrative trauma therapist in private practice outside of Baltimore. "Mistakes are how we learn." [76]

---

76 Margarita Tartakovsky, M.S., "A Powerful Exercise for Moving Past Regret," *PsychCentral*, September 11, 2017.

There have been many times in my life where I think, "*Damn! I wish I never did that.*" More times than I can count, I have beaten myself up over past situations. However, getting so worked up about things in the past did nothing for me except cause anxiety. I have worked through them, learned from them, and they no longer affect where I am in my life. I have now learned to leave the past in the past and only look toward my future.

"Hey, Wanna Go to the Movies?"

One of my regrets from college stems from something that happened my sophomore year. I met a guy in one of my classes who I was instantly interested in. After a little while, he seemed to be interested in me, too. He started talking to me and asked why he never saw me around before. One day, he asked me if I wanted to go to the movies with him. Unfortunately, I was sick the day of the movie and could not go. I was not blowing him off. I told him we could go another time.

Then, I found out one of my girlfriends liked him, too. I got so worried about what she would do if I went out with him that I ended up completely screwing myself over. Apparently, she had liked him for a while and told me how hurt she would be if I talked to this guy, let alone went to the movies with him. The thought of "*she won't be friends with me if...*" was something that never left my mind. Being a pleaser, I decided not to go out with him. I did not think about myself. Letting her stand in the way of what I wanted ruined my chance with this guy. Honestly, who knows—it probably would not have been anything, but it *might* have been something. I wish I would have been bold from the beginning and more assertive.

"If you work on your assertiveness, you will improve the quality of your relationships and you will enjoy them more...You can make sure that you don't waste your time on people who don't show you empathy." [77]

Sure, I have my flaws, but I am now confident in myself. One thing I now know is I will never change myself for anybody. It is important to remember the fact that no one is perfect and everyone has shortcomings. We all have our own imperfect pasts that have made us who we are today.

What Do I Want?

This situation in college made me realize I was doing everything for everyone else. I was not doing what I wanted to do. I got so mad at myself that I was sick and could not go to the movies. Then, when I was healthy and could have gone, it did not happen. If the roles had been reversed, the other girl would never have treated the situation the same way I did. I wish I would have been more assertive. Maybe if I would have said what was actually in my heart from the beginning, both relationships would have been different, but who knows. In the end, he didn't ask her out, either.

I was so worried about pleasing my friend that I did not even think of myself. This was not unusual. The thoughts of

---

77 "If You Try to Please Everyone, You'll Never Find What You Are Looking For," *Exploring Your Mind* (blog), June 15, 2018, accessed January 25, 2021.

others would always get in the way of what I wanted. I mean, yes, I should have talked to my friend and let her know how much I liked him, but I did not want to lose a friendship. That friendship ended up having a short lifespan, but how was I supposed to know at the time?

Not That Girl

Going back to my college days, there was a guy I thought was really hot. When we finally hung out, well, it was a one-time thing. I felt it was my fault as I did not let myself be perceived in the right way. As a consequence of my actions, I got so mad at myself because I felt dumb. I thought he actually wanted to get to know me. Clearly, I was wrong. Getting ghosted after that did not make me feel too great about myself. Eventually, I figured out that if guys did not want to spend the time getting to know me, why would I waste time on them?

Well, I made that mistake more than one time. One night, during my senior year of college, I went to the bar with some friends and was having a good time with them. We bar-hopped and I ended up drinking too much. My one friend knew this "well-known" guy who happened to be there with his friend, also considered well-known. She talked to the one she had met before, and I talked to the friend. Our other friends were doing their own thing and left us. I hit it off with the friend at the bar, and I wish I would have left it there. I was too drunk at the time, which did not help me make a good decision. Who knows if he would have ended up talking to me again or not? Regardless, I wish I would have made a different decision.

I came across an article on *Pop Sugar* that gives an accurate description of what I used to crave and who I used to be. No, I am not ashamed of myself for my past because I am who I am today because of it.

> *I developed a penchant for recklessness. I did not value myself; I told myself I didn't care. I became available to whomever wanted me, contorting myself mentally, emotionally, and physically for a brief chance at connection and fleeting approval. This pattern of self-destructive behavior continued for many years until I began to learn to love myself, finding beauty in my flaws and power in my intelligence and strength.* [78]

Forgive Yourself for the Past

Having men treat me badly always made me think it was a "me" thing. I thought I had to put up with the superficial treatment. It is a part of my past. I hope someone can learn from me. My confidence was at an all-time low and I so wanted the validation and attention of someone thinking I was pretty that I compromised much of who I was. I was told I was "hot" and had a good body, yet it made me feel like absolute shit. It was not a compliment. I felt like an object.

There are so many times I regret what happened. There are so many times I think I should not have done this or said that. Instead of getting stuck in those regrets, I have grown and am stronger from my mistakes. I am living my

---

78 Tess Chapin, "I Lost My Virginity During a One-Night Stand, and I Regret It," *Pop Sugar*, November 28, 2019, accessed January 24, 2021.

life and learning. I am not stuck in the past. It is perfectly normal to feel remorseful and have regret. That is a part of being human. I have found peace in what happened in the past and trust everything happened for a reason. I had to learn and accept it was okay to mess up and it was okay to not be perfect because perfection is not real. Ultimately, in the end I have become a stronger version of myself. Letting go of all the negativity and moving on with my life helped me better my mental health and overall well-being. There are small things you can do in order to help heal and give yourself forgiveness.

Forgiving yourself is tough. It means striking a deal with yourself:

to let the past be past and live in the present;

to stop beating yourself up about something that happened two or five or ten years ago;

to banish guilt and shame from controlling your thoughts and behaviors;

to accept and respect yourself as you are...in spite of your screw-ups. [79]

---

79 Anthony Centore, "How to Forgive Yourself: Letting Go of Past Regrets," *Thriveworks* (blog), April 9, 2015.

Lessons Learned

1. *Regret Is a Normal Feeling*

Learning and growing is how we better ourselves. Regret is a feeling I have felt a lot; however, I now try to use that regret as a learning experience to make better decisions. Taking these situations and learning from them has given me a chance to grow.

2. *Don't Blame Yourself*

My freshmen year of college was by far the worst one of my life. I was in a horribly depressed state. Even though I moved home and started at a new school and went to therapy, my life did not instantly become better. I was still struggling throughout most of my college career. I felt guilt all the time. My dad has even said he regrets telling me about the college where I first attended because that was where everything started to snowball. I tell him all the time, "Dad, you can't blame yourself or beat yourself up. It isn't your fault. Had I not had those experiences, I wouldn't be where I am now."

3. *Turn "I Wish I Never Did That" Into "I Won't Regret, I'll Learn"*

Have I messed up many times in my life? Yes. Does everyone? Yes. Do any of those situations define me? No. What defines me is my character and how I treat people with respect and care. People mess up. People say things and do things they wish they would not have done. When that happens, it is important to learn and grow.

4. Give Yourself Grace

It is easy to start blaming myself for everything I have done wrong; however, it is better to say, "I'm human. I messed up and I am learning." I feel much better by owning my mistakes and giving myself some grace instead of getting mad at myself. Grace is a game changer.

"Dianne Bondy, a yoga teacher and author of Yoga For Everyone, knows the saying well and is a 'big believer' in its potential. 'Grace happens to give us some space, acceptance, and room to take a hard swallow or step back...and practice self-compassion,' she says." [80]

5. Live for Today

We cannot go back and change the past. Forgive yourself and live for today. The only thing we can do is keep moving forward by learning and growing to become a better person.

How can you take your mistakes and turn them into something positive?

How can you learn and grow from your past?

---

80 Rebecca Ruiz, "What It Really Means to 'Give Yourself Grace,'" *Mashable*, November 21, 2020.

CHAPTER 10

Appreciate Yourself

———

Rejection: The dismissing or refusing of a proposal, idea, etc. [81]

*Life is not about looks and fitting into a certain image to be considered "likable" and "attractive." Life is not about trying to get everyone else to approve of you. Trying to live that way destroys your soul. Getting validation from other people is nice, but we do not **need** it. Our approval should come from within us. We are all equally entitled to our opinions, and at the same time, our opinions do not always need to be said. It is better to look forward and not worry about what people think of you.*

"No, we are sorry. You didn't get in."

"No, I don't want to be with you."

"No, you didn't get that promotion."

———

81   *Oxford English Dictionary, s.v.,* "rejection (n.)," accessed January 22, 2021.

These are just a few common rejections we might face in life. The most common type of rejection I have faced personally is with guys. I used to think awful thoughts, thinking *I fucking suck* and *no one wants me*. I didn't deserve someone. I was ugly. *What is wrong with me?* These thoughts destroyed my confidence. I would not only get rejected, but I would heap further rejection on myself. I would think time and time again that the rejection was just a part of me. Working on my confidence has taken many years. I still have my days, but I have learned that rejection from others never touched my character and who I am as a person.

Psychology Today published an article by Jeffrey Bernstein, Ph.D., in which he says:

> *We put our hearts and egos on the line. Yet intimate relationships don't always go the way we want, which can leave us with complicated feelings like sadness, grief, anger, guilt, and resentment. We often find ourselves replaying old conversations and scenes with an ex-lover, or our family members, while wishing we could have a second chance—and a new outcome. Anger is usually the most identifiable and pronounced emotion when a relationship ends. You must keep in mind that underneath anger are usually feelings of hurt, fear, sadness, and shame.* [82]

Being confident in who you are and what you are is what it is all about. You do not need everyone else to tell you that you are pretty, handsome, or smart. You can do it yourself.

---

82 Jeffrey Bernstein, Ph.D., "Three Ways to Break Free of Your Past Relationship Baggage: Letting Go of the Past and Moving on to a Healthy relationship," *Psychology Today, Sussex Publishers,* June 9, 2017.

When you find that inner confidence in yourself you do not need validation from others. It took me living through high school and college to realize I only need myself for validation. Believing in myself did not come from anyone else but me. Instead of always asking others "What do **you** think?" I now try to ask myself, "What do **I** think?" You know yourself better than anyone else. Do not look for someone that you want to get to know until you are confident in who you are.

Emotions and Feelings

Expressing vulnerability is important in building lasting friendships and relationships. Sometimes vulnerability will lead you to heartbreak or rejection, but it helps you grow as well. Rejection makes you stronger and helps you become more resilient to obstacles. Trust yourself above all else because your intuition is there for a reason. You learn to be vulnerable but also protect your heart at the same time because being vulnerable can sometimes lead to grief. Understanding and appreciating vulnerability is something we all could use a little more of. If we did, maybe we would be more empathetic and caring toward each other. It is not bad to feel things or to have certain emotions. The real question here is why do we not let ourselves be more real with each other?

*Many of us weren't taught how to express our emotions freely. For whatever reason—maybe our home situation, maybe childhood trauma, maybe our parents didn't ever express their emotions either—we've grown up with habits embedded deeply into us to keep us stifled and bottled up...***Vulnerability is consciously choosing to NOT hide your emotions or desires from others.** *That's it. You just freely express your* *thoughts, feelings, desires, and opinions regardless of what others might think of you.* [83]

In becoming an adult, you learn by going through many trials and errors. Making mistakes happens often, but you learn and keep going. This definitely happened to me when it comes to guys. I mean, how hard is it to tell someone you are not interested or do not think it is going to work? It's hard hearing that, but "ghosting" someone or treating someone like absolute shit is immature. We need to be able to communicate and talk. *Really* talk. Instead, we hide our emotions and always seem to fake it. Why don't we just start by using words and discussing how you are feeling? Feelings are not bad.

Dr. Marina Harris states:

"If we ignore our feelings, we miss vital information. Noticing our feelings and what they tell us shows us the big picture. It can help soften the emotion to make it bearable. It can help direct us towards behavior that makes our life better...You might be able to numb the pain, but numbing the pain leads to a less joyful, less fulfilled life." [84]

Emotions and feelings are central to life in the first place. We have created stereotypes of how strong men are supposed to be and how emotional women are. With men, we don't let them be as vulnerable as they should be because they are

---

83   Mark Manson, "Vulnerability: The Key to Better Relationships," Markmanson.net, accessed January 22, 2021.

84   Marina Harris, Ph.D., "You Can't Run from Your Feelings, but You Can Actually Use Them to Build a Happier Life," *Medium*, September 19, 2020, accessed January 25, 2021.

supposed to be tough. We have continued that stereotype: guys are not supposed to cry. What are they supposed to do? Swallow tears? Absolutely not. Show your emotions. Express them just like the rest of us. You have one life to feel these feelings. You and I both know you are not heartless. You have a soul and feelings, so let yourself feel what you feel.

Be mindful that everyone has emotions and feelings. Be honest. Get rid of your ego or whatever you want to call it. It is not cute. It is not sexy. It does not make you more of a guy or girl; not respecting another person's feelings makes you an asshole. Period.

Obsessing over a certain situation or guy became a vicious cycle for me. I would drive myself insane and become completely down on myself. No one deserves to feel insecure because of someone or something. We all feel. We all have emotions. Embrace it. Have feelings. Have thoughts. Have emotions. They are what make us human. By not letting ourselves truly feel, we are lying to ourselves. It is only a matter of time before everything explodes to the surface. When you are depressed, you might feel numb to everything, but in all reality, you are numb because you are feeling sad and alone. Giving yourself a chance to feel is crucial to living life to the fullest.

I came across a Ted Talk by *Jane the Virgin* actor Justin Baldoni. In it, he was vulnerable with his emotions.

I've been pretending to be a man that I'm not my entire life. I've been pretending to be strong when I felt weak. Confident, when I felt insecure. And tough when really, I was hurting. I think for the most part I've just been just kind of putting on a show...I had to acquire this almost disgusted view of the feminine and since we were told that feminine is the opposite of masculine, I either had to reject embodying any of these qualities or face rejection myself. This is the script that we've been given. Right? Girls are weak and boys are strong. This is what's being subconsciously communicated to hundreds of millions of young boys and girls all over the world just like it was with me. Well, I came here today to say as a man that this is wrong. This is toxic and this has to end. [85]

Society's stereotype is if men do not act brave, they are soft and weak. Baldoni said he was first told as a kid what type of man he should become. He wanted to feel liked and accepted by other boys, so he put on a show.

Self-love

Self-love is the most important thing you need. It comes from loving yourself for what and who you are. Love has to come from yourself first and foremost before anything else. I finally became my happiest when I stopped chasing guys for validation. I was not "easy," but I craved attention from guys so much that I changed myself and compromised my own personal beliefs. Romantic relationships are not everything. Recognize that you do not need another person to be in your life for you to find love or be successful. It all starts with appreciating yourself. Continuing to appreciate yourself even when people come in and out of your life will make you a lot happier. I used to feel ashamed for anything and **everything**. One minute I

85   Justin Baldoni, "Why I'm Done Trying to Be 'Man Enough,'" TEDTalk, filmed November 2017 at New Orleans, LA, video, 15:22. Tedtalk.

felt a guy was interested in me, making me believe I was confident because he thought I was pretty, and the next minute I would be ghosted. When this happened, self-hate and picking myself apart began. I was so hard on myself. I blamed myself constantly, but as I have learned, blaming yourself does nothing except lead you down a negative and dark path. The only thing that matters is simply: **what do I think about myself?**

"The greatest thing in the world is to know how to belong to oneself."

~ MICHEL DE MONTAIGNE

I used to question myself all the time. I would self-doubt to the point of hating myself. Relationships are something I never had a lot of growing up. I did not always have the most friends, and guys never liked me or even asked me to dance in middle school. I was invisible. In high school, I got unasked to two dances. To say I did not feel like a lowlife would be a lie. I felt I was only going through the motions. As I got older, most of my friends were dating people and I was single and confused. I really wondered why I was never "it." I constantly was fixated on the fact that I did not have a boyfriend. I would "third-wheel" my friends. I would joke about it even though it hurt me because I did not understand what I was doing wrong. Maybe I was too fucked up for anyone to handle.

Too often we look to romantic partners as a method of establishing our worth. Studies have shown some people can feel worthless and incompetent following a romantic rejection, especially if we have been overlooked in favor of someone

else (Deri and Zitek, 2017)...We consciously view rejection as
a reflection of ourselves and a determinant of our worth. [86]

We settle constantly when we know we deserve to be treated better. I settled for most of my teen years. I settled for bullshit behavior and being treated like crap because, at the time, I felt that was all I deserved. I felt unworthy. I never should have felt that way, because my worth does not come from anyone else but me—your worth comes from you. Fill yourself with confidence and poise. The only people you should focus on are the ones who see you, not just for how you look, but for your heart and your character. Part of becoming an adult is knowing what you deserve and the treatment you will tolerate. Did I deserve to be ghosted as many times as I have in my life? No. Does it have any reflection on who I am as a person? No. Someone acting petty and rejecting you is not a reflection of you in the slightest. It is a reflection on them.

It also takes courage to admit when we're wrong, or when we've knowingly hurt someone. Ghosting is sometimes referred to as a form of cowardice: the refusal to acknowledge one's own misconduct. And cognitive dissonance may play a role as well. Our brains naturally focus on information that confirms a preexisting belief about something, even when other evidence indicates that we might be wrong. Ghosters... often go through elaborate cognitive gymnastics to convince themselves that what they do is totally fine. [87]

---

86 Manj Bahra, "Rejection Isn't Your Reflection," *Noteworthy - The Journal Blog (blog)*, *Medium*, June 9, 2019, accessed January 22, 2021.

87 Loren Soeiro, Ph.D., "Seven Essential Psychological Truths about Ghosting: Why 'Ghosting' Hurts So Much, Why People Do It, and How You Can Get over It," *Psychology Today*, February 25, 2019.

It is really important to recognize that we are who we are and accept it regardless of any situation. You are the prize. Whether someone sees it or not, you need to make sure you appreciate yourself. Never change yourself for someone or for something. Love yourself because living carefree is the only way to live a happy life.

"Many of us get stuck in that place of fear, doubt, and shame that holds us back from realizing our true potential. When we can accept that we are simply human, it becomes easier to accept who we are as individuals. All of us have something to offer this massive, abundant world. Yes, even you." [88]

Only Compare Yourself to Yourself

Trying to compare yourself and your life to someone else's is one of the worst things you can do. I used to do this every single day. Trying to be the best or look my best was something I always tried to do because I wanted to be "just as pretty" as other people. My freshman year of high school was when I would compare my looks and every little thing about myself to other girls the most. If I ever saw a beautiful girl on social media, I would immediately get down on myself and think about how I was not as pretty as them.

I would self-deprecate over and over again to the point where it became destructive. Society gives the impression that if we do not look a certain way, then we are not pretty or attractive/ handsome to others. Society made me so insecure that I felt

---

88 Shawn McKibben, "When You Begin to Accept Yourself, These 10 Amazing Things Will Happen," Lifehack, November 17, 2014.

forced to use makeup every day because I felt ugly without it. I used it as a mask and would pile it on instead of enhancing my natural beauty. Makeup is something that should make you feel confident no matter how much or how little you use, as long as it makes you feel good about yourself. Use it for yourself, not for anyone else.

Through every experience I have had, I have realized I needed to embrace and accept everything I was. I put so much value in social media and what others had to say about me. My depression started to spiral during my freshman year of high school. I felt like I had been thrown into a pack of wolves as I was coming from a small middle school to a big public high school. I had no confidence. I did not know many people. I tried so hard to fit in to so many different groups, but I never felt that people liked or accepted me for me.

It was not until recently when one of my friends said to me, "Someone else's beauty doesn't take away from yours." That's when I realized I did not need to compare myself to others. If I approved of who and what I was, that was all that mattered. She made me realize I needed to stop comparing myself because we are all different for a reason. Even the people you may think are "perfect" are not even close. Let's be real. No one is perfect. All that matters is that you are confident in yourself.

Lessons Learned

1. Rejection Happens

The number of times I have been rejected by guys are too many to count. When applying to college or for jobs, having schools or workplaces reject you is normal. Sometimes things do not work out the way you want, but remember, there are better things ahead.

2. *Expressing Feelings by Being Vulnerable*

Feelings are a crazy thing. You have feelings daily. How you are feeling mentally and physically requires feelings. When we talk about feelings with each other, we learn about ourselves. We all handle life differently, so it makes sense that we all handle our emotions differently. Remember, men have feelings, too.

> *In his book,* What Men Don't Tell Women about Business: Opening Up the Heavily Guarded Alpha Male Playbook, *Christopher Flett claims that men don't often exhibit emotion "because we are taught that it is weak to do so. Men don't cry! Or if we do, we'll rarely admit to it. The truth is that we do get emotional—we just don't show it. Our fathers pull us aside and tell us to be two-faced: a private face outside of the public eye, and a public face that shows no weakness."* [89]

3. *It Isn't Always a "You" Thing*

We are so quick to blame ourselves when something goes wrong that we never stop and say to ourselves, "I am enough! I am worth it." Remember the old saying, "When one door closes, a window opens."

---

[89] Audrey Nelson, "Why Don't Many Men Show Their Emotions?" *Psychology Today,* Sussex Publishers, January 24, 2015.

4. You Are the Prize

When things do not work out, believe better things will come together. It is about not expecting anything from anyone else and focusing on bettering yourself. Our lows teach us to appreciate the highs. Make sure you recognize that you deserve the best. You deserve *more*. You are the prize, so channel that into your inner confidence. No one deserves you more than yourself.

5. Be Confident in Yourself

Find confidence from within and channel it into positive energy for yourself. Life is much more fun when you are confident in who you are. I know for myself the more confident I have become in who I am, the happier I have become. I might be insecure some days because I am human, and we all have our days; however, I am much better at snapping myself out of it quicker and getting back to the healthiest and most confident version of me.

"Self-esteem is a confidence booster and a real game-changer. This is a gift no one else can give you. Maybe there will always be haters in this world, but you don't have to live as a victim of them. You can allow their opinion to be none of your business, and travel through your life to the beat of your own inner drum." [90]

What can you do to better your relationship with yourself?

---

90 Kristin van Tilburg, "Seven Easy Ways You Can Appreciate Yourself More," *Medium*, February 4 2019, accessed January 22, 2021.

CHAPTER 11

Be Your Own Person

—

Peer Pressure: A feeling that one must do the same things as other people of one's age and social group in order to be liked or respected by them. [91]

When we make our own choices, we need to think about one thing—what the consequences are—and then make decisions and take chances from within our heart. It is about what you want to do, not everyone else. Choices should be not be determined by what others think we want or pressure us into; peer pressure and forcing someone to do something never works out in the end. We need to think about ourselves and what is best for us individually. Pressuring people, especially teens (as I once was), all had to do with social status and wanting to be "cool" and "popular."

When I was a teen, I saw people being ridiculed for wanting or not wanting something considered "cool" and what everyone else was doing. A perfect example of this is sex. During my teen years, I saw time and time again girls be labeled

---

91 *Merriam-Webster, s.v.,* "peer pressure (n.)," accessed October 19, 2020.

as a "prude" if they did not want to have sex with someone, but if they did have sex, they were automatically labeled a "slut." On the other hand, guys got praised for wanting to have sex with someone and sleeping with as many girls as possible. It has become *normal* today to pressure each other into making **our** decisions. We lose sight of what **we** want. We do what everyone else is telling us to do. It is hard to go against the norm, but I now ask myself, *what do I want?* Yes or no, I choose for *me.*

> *According to a 2019 report from the Guttmacher Institute, an organization working to advance sexual and reproductive health and rights, 65 percent of eighteen-year-olds have had sexual intercourse. That number jumps quite a bit—to 93 percent—when we get to twenty-five-year-olds. But that still leaves seven out of every 100 people in their mid-to-late twenties who haven't had sexual intercourse. The numbers continue to decline, but celibacy into one's thirties and forties is not unheard of.* [92]

Sex is an uncomfortable topic to discuss with our parents and schools. It is important to be educated and aware of the consequences that can occur after we make a choice. We either say yes to something or we say no. "Maybe" ultimately leads to a yes or no. Either way, it is in everyone's best interest to discuss the elephant in the room. As a teen, it is not as evident that people could be telling you something solely to protect you. You have to remember that your choices are

---

92 Judi Ketteler, "Many Teens Don't Have Sex. So Why Do Older Virgins So Often Feel Ashamed?" *Think: Opinion, Analysis, Essays*, NBC News, December 12, 2020.

your choices. Once they are made, they cannot be undone. Actions have consequences.

If someone does not respect your choices, that is a more serious issue. You need to think again about your relationship with that person and if being around them is healthy for you. You need to make choices based on what you know and want to do. When we are growing up, we think we need to act a certain way, when in reality we are putting ourselves more at risk. Conversations centered around sex are going to happen. Avoiding them will not do anything except increase the stigma around the conversation and cause more issues in the aftermath.

> *Unfortunately for adults hoping to avoid awkward conversations with banana stand-ins, this means doing away with abstinence-only programs. A review of the scientific literature found that these programs contain "scientifically inaccurate information, distort[ed] data on topics such as condom efficacy, and [promotion] of gender stereotypes." It concluded that abstinence-only programs put teens at greater risk of unintended pregnancies and STDs. With the gap between sexual maturity and marriage ever widening, such programs, no matter how well-intended, are simply unrealistic.* [93]

Mentally and physically, it is important to be healthy and safe. Reckless behavior can incur worse outcomes involving STDS and unplanned pregnancies. Not to mention, it can

---

93 Kevin Dickinson, "Sex, Condoms, and STDS: CDC Warns about Teen Risk Behaviors," *Big Think*, September 2, 2020.

put someone in an unfathomable state of mind. It is crucial we talk about subjects we are uncomfortable with, because once we open up, a discussion gives people a chance to obtain knowledge and act less impulsively.

Vodka, Tequila, Wine? Never Again

Going to bars and parties can be fun here and there, but it can also become repetitive. If someone offers you a drink, do not take it if you do not know them. On the other hand, if someone says they will buy you a drink, watch the bartender make it and then have the bartender hand it to you **directly.** This will ensure no one has touched your drink other than the bartender. You never know what people's intentions are, so it is better to be safe than sorry.

> *According to the Office on Women's Health, date-rape drugs like Rohypnol, GHB, and ketamine are used because they are not easily detected, and victims often do not remember being drugged or assaulted until many hours later. In 2016, there were over 320,000 incidents of rape and sexual assault, and these incidents are often underreported for both women and men. According to RAINN, 11.2 percent of college students experience rape or sexual assault through force, violence, or incapacitation, and in terms of drug-facilitated sexual assault, alcohol is the number one substance for assailants, next to prescription drugs with tranquilizing effects and Rohypnol, ketamine, GHB, and ecstasy.* [94]

---

94 "Spiked Substances," American Addiction Centers, accessed September 14, 2020.

During college, I focused so much on fitting in that I drank a lot. I learned to take shots instead of drinking a mixed drink most of the time. I pretended I could down those shots and keep up with everyone around me. I was not thinking about how sick I would get later on, especially knowing some of the other people were going to be perfectly fine the next day.

One of my best friends turned twenty-one right before Christmas, and I decided why not go all out with her because I wanted her to have a good birthday. We started the night by going out to dinner at one of our favorite restaurants. While we were there, we drank wine, then went to a bar and took green tea shots. As if we had not mixed enough alcohol already, we ended up at another place where we drank tequila shots and lastly, we went to a house party and drank beer. We drank so much and mixed so many things that the next day we both were extremely ill. That was probably the sickest I had ever been from drinking.

Her birthday was on December twenty-third, and Christmas was in two days. I was sick on Christmas Eve, as was she. For days after, I was sick to my stomach. The biggest consequence other than the illness was ruining the holidays with my family. The Mayo Clinic states what a normal amount of alcohol consumed looks like.

The more you drink, especially in a short period of time, the greater your risk of alcohol poisoning. One drink is defined as:

Twelve ounces (355 milliliters) of regular beer (about 5 percent alcohol)

Eight to nine ounces (237 to 266 milliliters) of malt liquor (about 7 percent alcohol)

Five ounces (148 milliliters) of wine (about 12 percent alcohol)

1.5 ounces (44 milliliters) of eighty-proof hard liquor (about 40 percent alcohol)

Mixed drinks may contain more than one serving of alcohol and take even longer to metabolize. [95]

Scary Reality

While in these types of social settings, it is important to stay in control; otherwise, it puts you in a vulnerable state, and someone could take advantage of you. Going into the teen and young adult years, it is important to be aware and cautious. When you are a teen, you are not thinking about what will happen tomorrow. You are not thinking of what the consequences might be from a particular action. Do not be naive. I sure was.

"On average, there are 433,648 victims (age twelve or older) of rape and sexual assault each year in the United States." [96]

Looking out for yourself is important when going out. Sure, some friends will take care of you, but others will not. One thing I had to learn was I have a low tolerance to alcohol.

---

95   "Alcohol Poisoning," Mayo Clinic, accessed January 27, 2021.
96   "Victims of Sexual Violence: Statistics," RAINN, accessed September 14, 2020.

Every time I would excessively drink, I would get sick for days. I prevented myself from having a productive day after one of those nights because all I wanted to do was sleep in my bed and drink a ton of Gatorade. I was flat out miserable. Eventually, drinking became something I did not want to do if it involved binge drinking because it can lead to some pretty terrible consequences.

When going out to a party/club/bar, be aware! If you happen to put your cup down, get a new one! I have been out several times where I have put my drink down and I either get a new one or do not get a drink at all. It is way better to be safe than sorry. If you ever see suspicious activity or something does not feel right, follow your intuition. *As they say at the airport: if you see something, say something.*

"Every ninety-eight seconds, someone in the US is sexually assaulted. That means every single day more than 570 people experience sexual violence in this country." [97]

"You Broke It How?"

Drinking too much has never ended too well for me. When I did, it turned into an absolute shitshow. October of my senior year, my roommate and I decided to plan a trip to a music festival called *Austin City Limits* in Austin, Texas. We landed the day before the festival. We rented a car (yes, some places will rent a car to people who are under twenty-five) and started driving.

---

97 Alanna Vagianos, "30 Alarming Statistics That Show the Reality of Sexual Violence in America: This is What an Epidemic Looks Like," *Huffpost*, updated April 6, 2017.

The next day my roommate and I got to the festival. We had "pre-gamed" before we got there. Since it was such a huge crowd, it did not take long before I lost her. I was standing there, wearing her hat, when a bunch of people started shoving each other and knocked the hat off my head. I do not know how, but when I bent down to try to save it, the hat was gone. People were still shoving and pushed me over and I landed on my hand. When I stood up, she was nowhere to be found, and my hand was swollen. I was in so much pain.

I knew something was seriously wrong, so I found the closest person that would help me. I was taken by golf cart to the emergency tent in the back of the music festival. The doctor working there told me I needed to get it immediately X-rayed. I was in Austin, Texas, had no car, and could not find my friend. I had to Uber myself to the hospital and sit in the emergency room for hours before I found out my hand was broken. I got a splint until I saw a doctor back at home.

The second day of the festival, we did not go. Instead, we decided to explore the city (which was fun except for my excruciating pain). On day three, I went to the concert in my splint. I knew I had to be extra careful, but I did not want to miss another day. I stayed sober the rest of that trip and that was fine with me. I have come to terms with the fact that I am more of the "mom" with my friends. I would much rather be taking care of them than having them take care of me. Being safe and aware with the right people when going out is important.

It's important for me to be surrounded with trustworthy people and real friends when going out. Truthfully, I do not need alcohol to have fun, but occasionally I love a wine night with friends because Moscato is one of the few alcohols I like. It's one thing to have friends over to casually hang out with a couple of drinks, but it is a different story to go out with the intent of getting as drunk as possible. In being the "mom," I have a different experience. It is a better experience, not to mention much safer being in control of yourself.

Lessons Learned

1. *Make Your Own Choices*

We all have the power over our own decisions, which means it is better to think through the consequences before being impulsive. No one should ever pressure or manipulate you into doing something you do not want to do. Being in social situations, it is extremely easy to let the peer pressure get the best of you. This has happened to me quite often. Drinking excessively is not exactly my idea of fun, and yet, I let my own thoughts and beliefs be pushed to the side so I could fit in with the crowd. Now, I do what I want and what I believe in my heart is right for me.

2. *Never Mix Alcoholic Drinks*

I will never mix any alcohol ever again. I have learned a hard lesson by how sick I got. Now, I cannot binge drink, which is fine because I do not even like the taste of most alcohols. Stick to one type of alcohol—that's my philosophy.

3. Sexual Assault Is More Common Than Most Would Think

Assault and abuse happens far too often. Drinking too much can impact judgment and someone might potentially take advantage. Definitely watch your drink so you do not get roofied. After seeing some friends in abusive relationships, I can say it is terrifying.

For crisis and counseling services, call the National Domestic Violence Hotline at 1-800-799-7233 or TTY 1-800-787-3224. [98]

4. Not Only is Sexual Assault Common, It Can Effect the Victim Mentally

Assault can make a victim sad and depressed. It is not uncommon for a victim to suffer from anxiety, as assault can have lasting effects after the fact.

Sexual assault can have a variety of short- and long-term effects on a victim's mental health. Many survivors report flashbacks of their assault, and feelings of shame, isolation, shock, confusion, and guilt. People who were victims of rape or sexual assault are at an increased risk for developing: depression, PTSD (Post-Traumatic Stress Disorder), substance use disorders, eating disorders, and anxiety. [99]

---

98 "Domestic Violence Resources," Live Your Dream.Org, accessed January 21, 2021.

99 "Sexual Assault and Mental Health," Mental Health America, accessed January 27, 2021.

5. *Always Watch Your Drink*

It is vital to make sure the drink in your hand stays in your hand. Whether at a bar or a party, drinks can get roofied if not properly watched. If you put it down, get another! If you do not like drinking and do not want to drink, realize you do not always need to have a glass in your hand.

"Fifty-one percent of men and 46 percent of women reported having drinks or food spiked at a house party." [100]

Alcohol isn't my favorite thing and if it isn't yours, embrace it. Drink a soda or water. Who cares! I like soda far more than I like alcohol and that is okay by me. Coca-Cola anyone?

---

100 "Spiked Substances," American Addiction Centers, accessed September 14, 2020.

PART 4

CHAPTER 12

Life Never Goes as Planned

Adaptability: The quality of being able to change or be changed in order to deal successfully with new situations.[101]

Life is a constant climb. All throughout life we learn. We make mistakes. We laugh. We cry. Sometimes our life does not turn out the way we thought it would. Taking life as a chance to experience something great happens by living each day to the fullest. Sometimes something unexpected happens that we would not have even imagined and sometimes we are not prepared for what is coming next.

Nothing in life was or is ever going to be perfect. The most important thing to learn is how to adapt. We have no idea what tomorrow will bring, nor can we control it. We must adapt to whatever will be thrown our way. Life is a weird thing. You

---

101 *Oxford Learner's Dictionary, s.v.,* "adaptability (*n.*)," accessed February 8, 2021.

might have your "plan" all set and ready to go, but then life might catch you off guard and change it completely. More often than not, my life has not gone the way I expected it to. When we have high expectations, we can be disappointed when they are not met. The most important thing we can do is adapt.

It had been months since the car accident, and I was in a lot of pain. I was not fully healed. In the midst of it all, my knee was throbbing and affecting my daily life. I was told I needed to get more treatment for it. My physical health became more important than anything else. I suddenly had to stop and make sure I was fully taking care of myself. I had thought moving was best for me, and I had a job offer set to go when I had to accept that I was supposed to stay exactly where I was to get better.

Having a plan is not a bad thing, it just means sometimes it could get interrupted. It does not set you back, it means there is a different path ahead for you. It is important to be content and present with where you are. Always trying to get to the next best thing makes you miss out on what is right in front of you.

> When you plan things out, you create expectations for the future. You want the future to play out in the way you planned and then most likely worry about what will happen when things don't go the way you planned...having a general plan can be useful because it's important for you to have as a reminder to look back on as you make progress. However, planning out the littlest of details is time consuming and the trade-off usually isn't worth it.[102]

---

102 Paul Hudson, "Be Spontaneous: The 6 Reasons You Should Never Make a Plan Again," *Elite Daily,* January 21, 2014.

Adaptability

The need for adaptability is everywhere. I had the chance to talk with Colleen McFarland, the author of *Disconnected*.[103] She told me how adaptability has become a major focus with young adults entering the work force. These people are extremely tech savvy and know how social media works, while older generations have to adapt to this tech-focused environment. The younger generations are more adaptable in using technology since they have been using it throughout their education and are used to being in front of a screen. The younger generation is constantly consuming data, using technology as a utility.

I had an internship at a small start-up where I was in charge of the company's social media presence. I made sure I was posting to different platforms to determine where they were getting the most traction. The company environment was more laid back since everyone in the company was in their late twenties and early thirties. It was a completely different environment from the large, established companies where I had other internships.

McFarland also discussed that people similar to her are trying to change how they manage the workplace and adapt to the younger crowd. She said it is important to be able to help the younger generation, which she called "Igens" (Millennials), adjust to the work environment. The Igens are the ones

---

103 Colleen McFarland, *Disconnected: How to Use People Data to Deliver Realness, Meaning, and Belonging at Work*, New Degree Press, 2020.

who possess technology skills to help everyone be successful in the workplace.

"You use tech, don't let tech use you."

~COLLEEN MCFARLAND

Tech uses us when we become too engrossed in it and forget why we are using it in the first place. Being so connected through social media has impacted social skills as well. With technology, people relate to each other differently than they would in a face-to-face interaction. In her book, McFarland references observations by Sanjay Kirtikar, a technology executive, who claimed that social media is ruining social skills.

> *His observation is that workers seem to be struggling with having productive verbal conversations at work. Research backs up Sanjay's claim. It shows that many are more comfortable communicating via words and emojis on their phones than face-to-face with words from their mouth. They know the right emoji to use in text, but don't always know the right facial expression to use, which of course means they don't know how to read those facial expressions as well either.* [104]

My generation has stress in performing verbal tasks. We constantly desire social approval and want more constant feedback from our managers on our performance. We want to make sure we have job security. By giving

---

104 Ibid., 117-118.

approval and training to this generation in these other tasks, employers are hoping to alleviate anxiety and keep it from escalating.

"They have been socialized that when they post something, everyone can weigh-in on it." [105]

Taking care of the mental health of young people, not only when they enter the workplace, but also throughout their careers is important. McFarland discussed wellness issues regarding mental health. We need to have a more open environment for people to be able to share their emotions and feelings. If a co-worker is mistreating another, there needs to be a conversation and a solution provided to the conflict. This technique can be used with someone in your everyday life as well. We need to use technology more positively, especially while we are in the workplace. We all deserve to come to work in a positive environment. Everyone deserves to feel calm and at ease without feeling stressed and emotionally drained because of each other and technology.

Plans Change

Adapting has never been the easiest thing for me, considering change can be scary. My sister always knows what to say to make me feel more at ease.

"Expect nothing, gain everything."

~JORDAN SKOWRON

---

105 Ibid., 132-133.

Before the pandemic was on the rise, I was a second-semester senior in college. I found out a course I needed to graduate was canceled. I was in a panic, because of course that was going to be taken from me! I had taken summer classes, had three internships, and was working my hardest so I could graduate in four years, which was my goal from the start. I got this email and my world came to a crashing halt. It meant no graduation for me.

"Hello Carolyn,

The University Registrar's Office has been directed to cancel IND123, Prototyping & Design for Product Development, for the upcoming second seven-week spring term. This course has been removed from your schedule. Please speak with your advisor if this requires additional changes to your semester registration."

This email tore my heart apart. I immediately freaked out. I was not going to walk across the stage. I dreamed about getting my diploma and moving my tassel to the other side. I was a girl who had been doubted all her life, and knowing I learn differently made me want it even more. I had to prove to myself I could accomplish what others had doubted I could. I was crushed, so I sent an email to the dean of my school.

"I have worked diligently and tirelessly to achieve this milestone by even taking summer classes. I will be empty inside knowing that I will still have work to do. My dream of graduating from Chatham will tarnished by walking across that

stage while still knowing that my classwork is not completed. I know that some might not think it's a big deal but graduation day has always represented to me the closure of becoming a college graduate."

Yes, I made a typo in my email. I dropped the "be" that should have been before tarnished. What I wanted to express was how important this was to me. I did get my point across, regardless of the grammar error. Everyone has sent out an email with a typo at one point or another. We are human, and we make mistakes.

I was relieved after I sent that email because I had done everything I could to plead my case. My college was amazing and figured out a way for me to still graduate by adding a special course to my schedule. I was excited we found an answer. I did an independent study with a wonderful and understanding professor. My advisor helped me so much through that whole process. I am so thankful for both of them. When I told my advisor how worried I was, she immediately sent emails and made calls to make sure I would walk across that stage.

I had a plan and a path to completion, but COVID-19 said otherwise, and I was crushed.

Graduation Made More Special

It only took one second for everything to change. Suddenly, my graduation was canceled. I was devastated. I wanted to walk across that stage so badly. I wanted to hold that diploma in my hand and move that tassel. I wanted to have that moment, which now would never happen. However, I got a moment that was even better all because of:

My sister.

She knew how upset I was. I walked upstairs one afternoon, and she said to me:

"Here, put this over your dress."

"What? How did you get this?"

"Put this cap and gown on, don't come downstairs yet."

"Okay, but why?"

"You will see."

She ran off while I was hanging out in the kitchen with my mom and dad. I was quite confused and had no idea what she was doing when she told me to come downstairs. I walked down the steps. She had somehow transformed our basement into a special ceremony. She had made a podium for me and decorated the room. She had chairs lined up (but socially distanced) as they would be at a graduation ceremony, and in the chairs were some of my friends who had snuck into the house without my knowing. For my "commencement speaker," my sister had found a video of Barack Obama giving a commencement address. It was a great speech. She played Master of Ceremonies and called my name and had me walk up in front of everyone. She handed me a diploma she had made, and I got to move my tassel to the other side of my cap.

It was special and one of the nicest things anyone had ever done for me. Even though I did not get to walk across the official commencement stage, I walked across the carpet with the closest people in my life cheering me on. It did not matter that I did not get what I wanted, because what I got was even better: I got to spend time with my family and friends celebrating my accomplishment.

Though the class of 2020 did not get to graduate in a normal way, we certainly did get to be creative with our loved ones and spend time with them celebrating what we did. It did not matter that none of us walked. We accomplished an incredible goal and *that* is what is important.

Life never goes the way you planned; life goes the way that it was supposed to go.

Enjoy the Journey

You might think you need to be somewhere else, but have you ever thought that you might already be where you need to be? It is better to enjoy the journey than to fight it. Everyone's journey is going to be different because we are all unique. No matter where I am, I can focus on being the best version of myself. I have learned that most things do not go according to plan. It works out the way it is supposed to.

Things do not always go the way we want them to. As much as it might throw you off, all it does is create a whole new plan that is better for you in the long haul. The only thing we have control over is how we respond to it. Going with the flow as best as we can allows us to appreciate life and live more in the moment, savoring more of the precious things that happen each day.

I had the pleasure of talking with Jaclyn DiGregorio, best-selling author of *Stop Getting in Your Own Way* [106] and *The Cusp Method*. [107] Jaclyn is someone who has made her life what she wanted it to be. She focused on what she had to do in the present to better her life and said it all started at an internship one summer where she was not fulfilled. She was at her internship one day and thought, "Is this really it?" That spark made her change her life completely.

She wanted to help others. She decided she wanted to do something more. She now is a life coach as well as motivational speaker. Her focus is to help women create the life they really want. She helps women plan but she focuses on the present. Jaclyn has a very positive outlook on life and does her best to use her knowledge and experiences to help others achieve their goals and dreams. Jaclyn never planned she would have her own business, but now she does and is happier than ever. She never planned for her level of success, but it sure has paid off. Her life is even

---

106 Jaclyn DiGregorio, *Stop Getting In Your Own Way: A No B.S. Guide to Creating the Business of Your Dreams*, New Degree Press, 2019.

107 Jaclyn DiGregorio, *The Cusp Method: Your Guide to Balanced Portions and a Healthy Life*, New Degree Press, 2017.

better than she thought it would be. She often uses the phrase, "objects in motion," which means to get the ball rolling and go with it.

"If something doesn't work out, something better will come along."

~JACLYN DIGREGORIO

Live in the Now

Some of the best moments of life are unexpected surprises that make you see how insane life can turn out. Writing a book was not something I ever imagined I would do and has become one of the most fulfilling things I have ever done. I never would have thought I would look at life with such a different perspective. If you would have asked me a year ago if I would ever become an author, I would have said you were crazy. Fast forward and here we are. This is the wonderful crazy thing about life. Plans change and people change. Think about romantic relationships and relationships with others. We cannot plan the future—it just happens.

Life falls into place in one way or another. Truthfully, you never know who you are going to meet. People leave, and while some do not come back, others do. We do not know what the future holds. We have to live in the now.

The problem is because we want the plan to work so badly, we are blind to other opportunities that may come our way. Plans are only good if they are extremely flexible. If they

aren't, they will make you close-minded and you won't even
realize it...We are aiming at the ideal outcome, not the actual
outcome, and therefore, we often choose to ignore the full
reality of the situation. You can't plan for every possible turn
of events, but you can be well prepared to handle the major-
ity of them...Plans never work out exactly the way you hope
them to—there are always tweaks, turns and changes. We
can't possibly plan something out to the very last detail; yet,
we try anyway. [108]

Reaching Out to Others

We can only hope for another day since we are not guaranteed tomorrow. Every second, every minute, every hour is yours. Make the most out of thinking about someone you miss, even someone you have not talked to in a while. Never underestimate the power of calling or texting someone you might be thinking about. You can make someone's day and more than that, make someone know they are loved and worthy of life.

One of my favorite ways to show people I care and value them is by calling and leaving a message, so they know they are loved, and I am thinking of them. Sometimes I will send texts to my friends telling them something as simple as, "Hope you have a good day." You never know if someone could really use the extra encouragement.

---

108 Paul Hudson, "Be Spontaneous: The 6 Reasons You Should Never Make a Plan Again," *Elite Daily,* January 21, 2014.

In today's world of demanding work schedules and commitments, showing up for someone can seem daunting, exhausting, even seemingly impossible. Because we live in survival mode a lot of the time, reaching out and checking in with a friend can feel uncomfortable. I get that stopping for a minute or so throughout your day to make a call or send a text or email, asking, "Hey, how have you been?" or "I just wanted to let you know that I'm thinking about you" can feel uncomfortable or seems like one more thing to do. If you're able to move past the initial awkwardness, though, it's worth doing. [109]

An unexpected gesture can make someone smile. While I was in the process of writing this book, one night I got a notification from someone I had not talked to in a few years. It made me so happy. It was one of my friends from my sophomore year of college. I had not talked to her in two years because we had a falling out over something I can't even remember. I had posted something that day on my social media about my book, and I got a direct message from her telling me how proud of me she was. Just by her sending one simple message instantly reconnected us. The crazy thing is we ended up video chatting shortly after she reached out. We might have lost two years, but when I saw her, it was as though not a single thing had changed. That is when you know you have a solid friendship.

109 Saba Harouni Lurie, "The Power of Reaching Out: Showing Up for Others," Take Root Therapy, June 14, 2018, accessed October 25, 2020.

You can't plan life—you just have to live it.

Lessons Learned

1. Adapt to Life

Adapting to new situations in life is crucial in order to be happy and move through life in a positive way. Whether it is at work or every day, it is important to adapt to what gets thrown at you.

"To adapt to change you need to fully accept it. If you resist, your life will stand still. You'll be existing but not moving forward and thriving." [110]

2. Change Happens

No matter if we want it to happen or not, change does happen. As we grow older, we go through different life events. We learn about our likes and dislikes as well as what we truly want out of life.

We cannot avoid it and the more we resist change the tougher our life becomes.

"Change is the law of life. And those who look only to the past or the present are certain to miss the future."

~JOHN F. KENNEDY

---

110 Alfred James, "How to Adapt to Change When You Want to Resist," *Pocket Mindfulness* (blog), accessed October 26, 2020.

"*Change as John F. Kennedy quoted is a Law of Life. We are surrounded by change and it is the one thing that has the most dramatic impact on our lives. There is no avoiding change as it will find you, challenge you and force you to reconsider how to live your life.*" [111]

3. Enjoy the Journey, Not the Destination

There have been so many times in my life where I would get so get caught up in the final destination that I would miss out on the beautiful parts of life I was passing. This is what life is about. When life does not go as planned, it is because there is something different ahead.

4. If It's Meant to Be, It Will Be

When we think life will go one way and it then goes another, we get disappointed. That is why I'm now living my mantra: "if it's meant to be, it will be," because sometimes lessons and different experiences have to happen. Whether that be a relationship or job or friendship, I believe if something is meant to happen, it will. Life works best when it is not forced.

5. Reach Out to an Old Friend

A simple gesture can completely turn someone's day around. The amazing thing about writing this book was getting back in touch with so many people I had not talked to in years.

---

111 Kathryn Sanford, "Adapting to Change: Why it Matters and How to Do It," *Success Mindset*, Lifehack, January 12, 2021, accessed January 25, 2021.

We got the chance to reconnect. It is such a rewarding feeling when someone you have not talked to in a long time connects with you, and it's like nothing has changed. Letting people know they are loved, and you care about them can help with someone's mental health.

"Reuniting with a long-lost college roommate or a grade-school pal enhances one's well-being. Reminiscing about things you once did is actually a good thing." [112]

Who could you reconnect with that would benefit your mental health?

---

112 Meghan Holohan, "Reach Out to an Old Friend—Research Says It is a Mood Booster," *Mind & Body, Today*, April 30, 2020.

CHAPTER 13

You Are Unbreakable

———

Unbreakable: Not able to be broken.[113]

Do you ever feel like you are walking on glass and just seconds away from shattering? Be real with yourself and realize that life has never been perfect for anyone. It sometimes requires you to crash and burn before you can reach the top. Life has its good and bad moments, but remember, no one should ever feel isolated and alone. We all have been there. Whether you admit it to yourself or not, everyone has felt lonely and unworthy. It is time to thrive from within. Let's be open and honest with each other.

On the outside, it might have looked like "I had it all," but no one knew I was beyond broken and alone inside. Everyday felt like another one wasted. I had days where I would just have a breakdown in my room. I had days where self-harm was what I thought I deserved. My freshmen year of college nearly killed me. I had the feelings that I never fit in and I did not have a group of friends. Something was wrong with me since

———

113 *Merriam-Webster, s.v.* "unbreakable (adj.)," accessed October 29, 2020.

I never felt I belonged anywhere. I had great clothes, but I did not have a sense of worth. I was depressed and anxious daily. I became a shopaholic. Things I bought would make me feel better for a moment, but at the end of the day, it was just stuff.

"When we make a purchase and/or get what we want, we are temporarily happy and fulfilled. But the reason for happiness is not because we got what we wanted, but because for a brief period of time, we stopped wanting, and thus we experience peace and happiness." [114]

You never fully know what someone has going on in their life. There could be so much more going on than what you think. We each have a story. We may think we know a chapter or two and yet we forget there are several parts of each other's lives we have no idea about. We all struggle with something.

Revaluate

Being kind and respectful to each other is how the world could start becoming a better place. If you happen to think you are better or above someone else because of "who you are," seriously understand that is a bunch of bullshit. We all are on the same level and all deserve to have respect from and for each other. It does not matter who you are or what you stand for. It is not rocket science to be a person with dignity, kindness, and respect for others. No matter how much money is in your bank account, you are not better

114 Joshua Becker, "Nine Reasons Buying Stuff Will Never Make You Happy," *Becoming Minimalist* (blog), accessed October 30, 2020.

than anyone else. The number of followers someone has is not a reflection of character. This is the time to be different and treat each other as equals.

Degrading each other goes back to our mental health and how we view ourselves. Some people without good self-esteem think treating someone poorly makes them feel better about themselves. Are you being rude to someone who might actually be a nice person? One-night stands do not allow anyone a chance to show themselves for who they are, and honestly, how is this respectful behavior?

Live Science did a study about one-night stand realities. Why are we normalizing this? Seriously, one-night stands can completely mess with someone's self-esteem and dignity.

> *Among the findings: Women were not hooking up in an effort to secure a long-term beau, but because they felt flattered by the overnight proposition. They were mistaken. As the researcher points out, men lower their standards when it comes to one-night stands, so the presumed flattery is a fantasy or close to it. "No woman should be flattered because a man wants to have sex with her once." "If you've got a Brad Pitt character—absolutely gorgeous and incredibly loaded with money and so on—the chances of getting him to commit himself to you for the rest of your life are pretty slim," Campbell said. "But the chances of him giving you a half an hour on a Wednesday afternoon in a hotel are probably much better." [115]*

---

115 Jeanna Bryner, "Realities of One-Night Stands Revealed," *Live Science,* July 10, 2008.

Normalizing chivalrous and classy behavior will help people see that treating each other the way we deserve to be treated creates better feelings. Ask yourself:

Do you actually feel better about yourself or your ego living the life you do?

Does going from person to person make you feel "cool?"

Do you care for the person or is it strictly physical?

All I am saying is this: I have been in plenty of situations where the person cannot commit. Leading someone on is not necessary. Enough with the games. Be respectful.

Everyone Struggles with Something

The individuals most people would look at as "tough" and "strong" have their own fair share of issues as well. The Rock (also known as Dwayne Johnson), struggles with depression and expressed how important it is to talk about.

> *I found that, with depression, one of the most important things you could realize is that you're not alone," Johnson said during an episode of* Oprah's Master Class *on the OWN network. "You're not the first to go through it; you're not going to be the last to go through it…I wish I had someone at that time who could just pull me aside and [say], 'Hey, it's gonna be okay. It'll be okay.' I wish I knew that.* [116]

---

116 Sara Altshul, "Fourteen Celebrities Who Have Experienced Depression," *Everyday Health*, March 4, 2016, accessed September 13, 2020.

He was right when he said it will be okay. We can all be more open with each other and not be so judgmental or think topics are too "taboo." Instead of judging someone, think about this: the model who has a million "likes" is dealing with her dad having cancer; the cute guy you met in class is dealing with his parents' divorce; the girl with the prettiest smile tried to kill herself; the guy who ghosted you is dealing with depression. You never know what someone is battling in their own life. We all have issues, but we keep them so far hidden that sometimes we refuse to accept them until it is too late.

Imperfections Don't Break You, They Make You

"Open the doors that are meant to be open, close the doors that are meant to be closed."

~MADISON THOMAS

You are perfect the way you are. Learn to accept and enhance your natural beauty—accept your handsomeness. Let's face it: we are so self-critical. We see things that others do not see. I used to consider my nose a flaw since I was badly bullied for it. I hated wearing my hair up because I felt ugly, and my forehead was too big. Through time and learning to love myself, I now see myself how I am meant to be. Sure, I have my days of being down on myself, but I have learned to appreciate those days because they are a part of what makes me, *me*.

Every single one of us has flaws. That is just a fact. It might not in reality even be a flaw, but if you consider it so, you need to learn to embrace it.

I got to talk with Madison Thomas, the author of *Redefining*. [117] We talked about life and positivity. She shared her story of overcoming tough challenges and still looking at life positively. She has had thirty-two surgeries in her life and has scars on her left leg. She owns it and uses her story to help others feel more comfortable in their own skin. Madison's book is a perfect example of how beauty does not need to have a standard. She is defining beauty in a new way, which is all about real, natural, true beauty and how important it is for us to accept ourselves for who and what we are.

"I have learned just how much true beauty is something internal that is outwardly expressed from the heart."

~MADISON THOMAS

Be the Best You

As this book comes to a close, I hope everyone is well aware by now that no one is weak for having any sort of mental health issue. We all have days when we feel better than others. Why do we make fun of someone for crying or someone who is struggling but who doesn't have the courage to ask for help? You do not know what is happening behind closed doors, so let's give each other a little grace. We can all start by showing each other it is okay to struggle and it is okay to be different. Do not assume anyone "has it all," because the real fact is that none of us do.

---

117 Madison Thomas, *Redefining: What 32 Surgeries Taught Me about How to View Life and My Body*, self-published, 2020.

I know how easy it is to be in middle school, high school, and even college and want to change yourself to make others like you. Let me say this: do not change a thing about yourself. Dress how *you* want. Talk like *you*. Be okay with the fact that you are not perfect, because just like you, I am definitely not perfect either. No one is. We all make mistakes. We are all insecure about a part of ourselves from time to time, but that has no reflection on your worth. Try and look at yourself differently. Do not think you need to do this or that to get someone to like you.

As long as YOU are making decisions and living your life for you, the judgment of others means nothing. If you are klutzy like I am, laugh at yourself and be okay with it, since that is a part of you. I am not changing myself for anyone.

"In order to be irreplaceable one must always be different."

~COCO CHANEL[118]

Live Your Best Life

We only get one chance on this earth, so let's come together to create a new normal and celebrate ourselves for who we are. No matter what age or gender you are, you know this world needs a huge change, and it can only happen if we focus on the root of the problem. Pave your own path. Appreciate yourself for what you do have. Life is not about getting to the top; it is about appreciating where

---

118 Barry Samaha, "The Best Coco Chanel Quotes about Fashion, Love, and Success," *Harper's Bazaar*, June 25, 2020.

you are at that exact moment. I mean, do I dream for this book to become a bestseller? Yeah, absolutely! Who would not want that? However, what I am most grateful for is where I am now. I am in a much healthier place. The truth of the matter is that life is not about how many diamonds or houses you can buy—it is simply about love and appreciating the simple moments. Giving of your time and empathy are much bigger than anything else. That is what life is about.

Appreciate your own life and be generous if you can. You never know who you can help by even the smallest of acts. You can be a game changer and make someone's day. A simple act can be the one that saves someone's life.

Lessons Learned

1. *No One "Has It All"*

No matter what people have said about me in the past, I can surely say I do not have it all, and I never will. I am not perfect, and after reading this book, you know my life has never been perfect, either. I value my mental health over anything. It is about being around the people I love and the moments I can cherish and hold onto.

2. *Enough is Enough*

Treating people as human beings is not hard and yet, we make it seem that way. All of us have done this, but it is time we change. It is time we start living in a world that is more supportive and less about getting "status" from the myriad of ways people "see" status. None of that matters at the end of the day. What matters is who you are on the inside. Period.

"Only when you're finally able to say, 'enough is enough!' are you able to begin making the changes in your life that your heart and soul crave." [119]

3. Own Your "Flaws"

It is too easy to get down on myself, but I can embrace myself for who I am and what I can offer the world. Talking to other people lets me know I am not alone, and it is okay to embrace my flaws. No more need for filters. Embrace your imperfections because they are something we all have.

4. Your Story Is Worth Sharing

Writing this book has been the most "out of my comfort zone" thing I have ever done. Opening up and being unashamed of what I have gone through has been so important for my growth. Acknowledging what each one of us is going through is when we can start to bring this world together, one story at a time. We all have our personal journey that creates our very own story.

> *Stories are about collaboration and connection. They transcend generations, they engage us through emotions, and they connect us to others. Through stories, we share passions, sadness, hardships, and joys. We share meaning and*

---

119 Brian Thompson, "When Enough is Enough: Confronting the Ego," *Zen Thinking* (blog), November 19, 2015, accessed October 30, 2020.

purpose. Stories are the common ground that allows people to communicate, overcoming our defenses and our differences. Stories allow us to understand ourselves better and to find our commonality with others. [120]

5. You Are Unbreakable

Do not let anyone or anything stand in the way of what you want in life. Love and embrace yourself for who you are. If you still happen to be searching for your purpose or what you are passionate about, I always like to think of it as, *what makes me smile? What motivates me?* I still ask myself these questions. By trying to answer them, I get a better understanding of what I am trying to figure out. I am still trying to find my way. I know my value now, and I hope you have a better understanding of your worth, too.

Nothing is worth trying to end your story early. No matter what your age, you are only at the beginning. Don't you want to know what will happen during the next part of your journey and what the entirety of your book will look like?

You are enough. You are worth it. You are UNBREAKABLE.

---

120 Pamela B. Rutledge, Ph.D., "The Psychological Power of Storytelling: Stories Leap-Frog Technology, Taking us to Authentic Experience," *Psychology Today*, January 16, 2011.

Appendix

Introduction

Bailey, Alyssa. "Selena Gomez: 'I Had Everything, but I Was Broken Inside.'" *ELLE,* October 11, 2017. https://www.elle.com/culture/celebrities/news/a40930/selena-gomez-ama-acceptance-speech-2016/.

Cohen, Jennifer. "The Secret to Getting Anything You Want in Life." Filmed October 20, 2019 at TEDxBuckhead, Atlanta, GA. YouTube. Video, 16:01. https://www.youtube.com/watch?v=wM82hE6oimw.

Merriam-Webster, s.v. "Stigma (n.)." Accessed December 19, 2020. https://www.merriam-webster.com/dictionary/stigma.

National Institute of Mental Health. "Mental Illness." Last updated January 2021. Accessed January 31, 2021. https://www.nimh.nih.gov/health/statistics/mental-illness.shtml.

Chapter 1

American Academy of Child & Adolescent Psychiatry. "Threats by Children: When Are They Serious." No.65 (January 2019). https://www.aacap.org/AACAP/Families_and_Youth/Facts_for_Families/FFF-Guide/Childrens-Threats-When-Are-They-Serious-065.aspx.

Bayer, Casey. "When Kids Are Held Back, Gains Can Follow." *Usable Knowledge.* Harvard Graduate School of Education, July 2017. https://www.gse.harvard.edu/news/uk/17/07/when-kids-are-held-back-gains-can-follow.

Bologna, Caroline. "What Kids Who Bully Often Have in Common." *HuffPost,* August 30, 2019 6:57 p.m. EST. https://www.huffpost.com/entry/bullies-common-characteristics_l_5d668b39e4b063c341f8e4ba.

Bremner, J. Douglas. "Traumatic Stress: Effects on the Brain." *Dialogues in Clinical Neuroscience 8, no. 4 (*December 2006): 445-461. https://www.ncbi.nlm.nih.gov/pmc/articles/PMC3181836/.

Merriam-Webster, s.v. "Bullying." Accessed August 27, 2020. https://www.merriam-webster.com/dictionary/bullying.

Nicholson, Jeremy. "Should You Do What Everyone Else Is Doing?" *Psychology Today.* Sussex Publishers, March 31, 2019. https://www.psychologytoday.com/us/blog/persuasion-bias-and-choice/201903/should-you-do-what-everyone-else-is-doing.

Wilkins, Melissa Camara. "What It Means to Be Enough." Accessed January 4,2021. https://melissacamarawilkins.com/what-it-means-to-be-enough/.

Yagoda, Maria. "Shawn Mendes, Lady Gaga, & More Stars Who've Opened Up about the Bullying They Faced as Kids." *People,* November 20,2019. https://people.com/celebrity/bullying-rumer-willis-jessica-alba-jessica-simpson-and-eva-mendes/?slide=6231920#6231920.

Chapter 2

Apple Music. "Miley Cyrus—Apple Music 'Plastic Hearts' Interview." Interview by Zane Lowe. YouTube. November 23, 2020. Video, 1:19:24. https://www.youtube.com/watch?v=ffMN__YxLMI.

Haynes, Trevor. "Dopamine, Smartphones, & You: A Battle for Your Time." (blog), *Science in the News,* Harvard University the Graduate School of Arts and Sciences, May 1, 2018, accessed January 10, 2021. http://sitn.hms.harvard.edu/flash/2018/dopamine-smartphones-battle-time/.

Jarrett, Christian. "The 10 Toxic Psychological Traits That Make So Many People Suck." *Fast Company,* December 11, 2018. https://www.fastcompany.com/90278683/the-10-toxic-psychological-traits-that-make-so-many-people-suck.

Jhangiani, Rajiv, Hammond Tarry, and Charles Stangor. "Defining Social Psychology: History and Principles." *Principles of Social Psychology 1st*

International Edition. September 26, 2014. https://opentextbc. ca/socialpsychology/chapter/defining-social-psychology-history-and-principles/.

Kiersz, Andy and Allana Akhtar. "Suicide Is Gen Z's Second-Leading Cause of Death, and It's a Worse Epidemic Than Anything Millennials Faced at That Age." *Business Insider.* October 17, 2019. https://www.businessinsider.com/ cdc-teenage-gen-z-american-suicide-epidemic.

Kreager, Derek A. and Jeremy Staff. "The Sexual Double Standard and Adolescent Peer Acceptance." *Social Psychology Quarterly,* June 1, 2009. https://journals.sagepub.com/doi/ pdf/10.1177/019027250907200205.

McLean Hospital. "The Social Dilemma: Social Media and Your Mental Health." February 26, 2020. https:// www.mcleanhospital.org/news/it-or-not-social-medias-affecting-your-mental-health.

McSweeney, Kelly. "This is Your Brain on Instagram: Effects of Social Media on the Brain." *NOW,* March 17, 2019. https:// now.northropgrumman.com/this-is-your-brain-on-insta-gram-effects-of-social-media-on-the-brain/.

Merriam-Webster, s.v. "Status (n.)." Accessed August 30, 2020. https://www.merriam-webster.com/dictionary/status.

Chapter 3

Cortiella, Candace and Sheldon H. Horowitz. *The State of Learning Disabilities: Facts, Trends, and Emerging Issues.*

New York: National Center for Learning Disabilities, 2014. Accessed September 13, 2020. https://www.ncld.org/wp-content/uploads/2014/11/2014-State-of-LD.pdf.

Greene, Leana. "Overcoming the Shame of My Learning Disability." Kids in the House (blog). *Huffpost,* December 6, 2017. https://www.huffpost.com/entry/overcoming-the-shame-of-my-learning-disability_b_6803024.

Merriam-Webster, s.v. "Learning Disability (n.)." Accessed September 14, 2020. https://www.merriam-webster.com/dictionary/learning%20disability.

National Center for Learning Disabilities. "The State of LD: Understanding the 1 in 5." May 2, 2017. Accessed January 10, 2021. https://ncld.org/news/newsroom/the-state-of-ld-understanding-the-1-in-5.

Shulman, Michael. "One in Three College Freshmen Worldwide Reports Mental Health Disorder." American Psychological Association. September 13,2018. Accessed September 13, 2020. https://www.apa.org/news/press/releases/2018/09/freshmen-mental-health.

Smart Kids with Learning Disabilities. "Nonverbal Learning Disabilities: An Overview." Accessed February 1, 2021. https://www.smartkidswithld.org/first-steps/what-are-learning-disabilities/nld-overview/.

The Association of Boarding Schools. "The Big Picture on Boarding Schools." Accessed September 14, 2020. http://www.boardingschools.com/discover/bigpicture.aspx.

The NVLD Project/Nonverbal Learning Disability. "What is Nonverbal Learning Disability?" Accessed September 13, 2020. https://nvld.org/non-verbal-learning-disability/.

Chapter 4

American Psychological Association. "One in Three College Freshmen Worldwide Reports Mental Health Disorder." September 13, 2018. Accessed September 13, 2020. https://www.apa.org/news/press/releases/2018/09/freshmen-mental-health.

Gordon, Serena. "Kids Often Use OTC Drugs in Suicide Attempts." WebMD Archives. Originally published by HealthDay News, October 7, 2019. https://www.webmd.com/mental-health/addiction/news/20191007/kids-often-use-otc-drugs-in-suicide-attempts#1.

Iliades, Chris, M.D. "Depression's Effect on Your Appetite." *Everyday Health*, September 10, 2012. https://www.everydayhealth.com/hs/major-depression/depressions-effect-on-appetite/.

Kiersz, Andy and Allana Akhtar. "Suicide Is Gen Z's Second-Leading Cause of Death and It's a Worse Epidemic Than Anything Millennials Faced at that Age." *Business Insider*, October 17, 2019. https://www.businessinsider.com/cdc-teenage-gen-z-american-suicide-epidemic.

Kindelan, Katie. "On World Suicide Prevention Day, What 4 Survivors of Suicide Want You to Know." Good Morning America, September 9, 2019.

https://www.goodmorningamerica.com/wellness/story/life-attempting-suicide-survivors-55841545.

LeBlanc, Nicole J., M.A. and Luana Marques. Ph.D. "Anxiety in College: What We Know and How to Cope." *Harvard Health Blog,* (blog), Harvard Health Publishing, May 28, 2019. https://www.health.harvard.edu/blog/anxiety-in-college-what-we-know-and-how-to-cope-2019052816729.

Merriam-Webster, s.v. "Isolate (s.v.)." Accessed September 10, 2020. https://www.merriam-webster.com/dictionary/isolate.

Purse, Marcia. "What is Suicidal Ideation? A Look at Dangerous Thought Patterns." *Very Well Mind.* Dotdash, March 25, 2020. https://www.verywellmind.com/suicidal-ideation-380609.

Searing, Linda. "The Big Number: 1 in 3 College Freshmen Show Signs of Mental-Health Disorders." *The Washington Post.* WP Company, September 25, 2018. https://www.washingtonpost.com/national/health-science/the-big-number1-in-3-college-freshmen-show-signs-of-mental-health-disorders/2018/09/21/ea7b1fd8-bcf0-11e8-8792-78719177250f_story.html.

Chapter 5

Fairchild, Mary. "What God's Grace Means to Christians: Grace Is the Undeserved Love and Favor of God." Learn Religions. Dotdash publishing, updated June 25, 2019. Accessed January 14, 2021. https://www.learnreligions.com/meaning-of-gods-grace-for-christians-700723.

"Gratitude Journal (Greater Good in Action)." *Greater Good in Action—Science-Based Practices for a Meaningful Life.* University of California Berkeley. Accessed September 29, 2020. https://ggia.berkeley.edu/practice/gratitude_journal.

Hammel, Jess. *National Alliance on Mental Illness (NAMI) Zoom presentation to Mt. Lebanon High School students. November 30, 2020.*

Herbst, Diane. "Kevin Hines Survived a Jump Off the Golden Gate Bridge—Now, He's Helping Others Avoid Suicide." *Psycom.* Remedy Health Media, last updated September 9, 2019. Accessed January 14, 2021. https://www.psycom.net/kevin-hines-survived-golden-gate-bridge-suicide/#kevin-sstory.

Mental Health America. "Mental Illness and the Family: Recognizing Warning Signs and How to Cope." Accessed September 18, 2020. https://www.mhanational.org/recognizing-warning-signs.

Merriam-Webster, s.v. "Purpose (n.)." Accessed September 15, 2020. https://www.merriam-webster.com/dictionary/purpose.

Pombo, Emmie. "Self-Help Techniques for Coping with Mental Illness." National Alliance on Mental Illness. February 1, 2019. https://www.nami.org/Blogs/NAMI-Blog/January-2019/Self-Help-Techniques-for-Coping-with-Mental-Illness.

Smith, Melinda, M.A., Lawrence Robinson, and Jeanne Segal, Ph.D. "Depression Symptoms and Warning Signs." Help Guide, last updated September, 2020. Accessed September

20, 2020. https://www.helpguide.org/articles/depression/depression-symptoms-and-warning-signs.htm.

Yasin, Kareem. "This Is What Suicide Survivors Want You to Know," *Healthline*, updated on December 20,2019. https://www.healthline.com/health/mental-health/what-suicide-survivors-want-you-to-know#2.

Chapter 6

Botkiss Center for Recovery. "Are Intensive Outpatient Treatment Programs the Future of Mental Health?" August 28, 2019. Accessed January 15, 2021. https://botkissrecovery.com/2019/08/28/are-intensive-outpatient-treatment-programs-the-future-of-mental-health/.

Bradley University. "How to Overcome the Cultural Stigma Surrounding Counseling." Accessed January 14, 2021. https://onlinedegrees.bradley.edu/blog/how-to-overcome-cultural-stigma-surrounding-counseling/.

Brady, Krissy. "Thirteen Signs You Are Sabotaging Your Own Progress in Therapy: Therapists Reveal How to Know If You Aren't Getting the Most Out of Your Therapy Sessions and How to Fix It." *Huffpost*, September 19, 2019. https://www.huffpost.com/entry/signs-sabotaging-therapy-progress_l_5d40ac12e4b0db8affafb0a2.

DeVries, Katherine. "Tips for Talking to Someone About Self-Harm." Pine Rest Christian Mental Health Services. Accessed February 1, 2021. https://www.pinerest.org/tips-for-talking-to-someone-about-self-harm-blog/.

Merriam-Webster, s.v. "Empathy (n.)." Accessed October 1, 2020. https://www.merriam-webster.com/dictionary/empathy.

Smitha Bhandari, M.D. "Dialectical Behavioral Therapy." WebMD, February 18, 2020. Accessed January 14, 2021. https://www.webmd.com/mental-health/dialectical-behavioral-therapy#1.

Chapter 7

Collins, Ryan. "Exercise, Depression, and the Brain." *Healthline*, Healthline Media, July 25, 2017. https://www.healthline.com/health/depression/exercise.

DeAngelis, Tori. "Who Self-Injures." American Psychological Association, July/August 2015, Vol 46, no. 7. https://www.apa.org/monitor/2015/07-08/who-self-injures.

Hull, Megan, editor. "Self-Harm Statistics and Facts." The Recovery Village, updated December 23, 2020. Accessed January 17, 2021.

https://www.therecoveryvillage.com/mental-health/self-harm/related/self-harm-statistics/.

Jaffee, Jaelline, Ph.D, Lawrence Robinson, and Jeanne Segal, Ph.D. "Are You Feeling Suicidal?" HelpGuide.org, updated September 2020. Accessed September 13, 2020. https://www.helpguide.org/articles/suicide-prevention/are-you-feeling-suicidal.htm.

Lang, Susan S. "Self-Injury Is Prevalent among College Students, but Few Seek Medical Help Study by Cornell and Princeton Researchers Finds." *Cornell Chronicle,* June 5, 2006. https://news.cornell.edu/stories/2006/06/self-injury-prevalent-among-college-students-survey-shows.

National Alliance on Mental Illness. "Self-Harm." Accessed October 16, 2020. https://www.nami.org/About-Mental-Illness/Common-with-Mental-Illness/Self-harm.

Oxford Learner's Dictionary, s.v. "Self-Harm (n.)." Accessed February 1, 2021. https://www.oxfordlearnersdictionaries.com/us/definition/english/self-harm_1?q=self+harm.

Sunshine Behavioral Health. "Coping Strategies & Addiction: Recovery Skills and Tools for Coping." Accessed October 15, 2020. https://www.sunshinebehavioralhealth.com/addiction/coping-with-addiction/.

Whitlock, Janis, Stephen P. Lewis, Imke Baetens, and Penelope Hasking. "Non-Suicidal Self-Injury on College Campuses." *Higher Education Today (blog).* American Council on Higher Education, February 6, 2019. https://www.higheredtoday.org/2019/02/06/non-suicidal-self-injury-college-campuses/.

Chapter 8

Beck, J. Gayle and Scott F. Coffey. "Assessment and Treatment of PTSD after a Motor Vehicle Collision: Empirical

Findings and Clinical Observations." U.S. National Library of Medicine, May 28, 2008. https://www.ncbi.nlm.nih.gov/pmc/articles/PMC2396820/.

MADD. "Statistics: Fight Back against Misinformation. Get the Facts." Accessed January 24, 2021. https://www.madd.org/statistics/.

National Highway Traffic Safety Administration. "Alcohol Impaired Driving." November, 2018. Accessed February 2, 2021. https://crashstats.nhtsa.dot.gov/Api/Public/ViewPublication/812630.

Oxford English Dictionary, s.v. "Consequence (n.)," accessed January 24, 2021. https://www.lexico.com/en/definition/consequence.

Prince, Ruth E. C. "Connections, Consequences, and Understanding: Encouraging Teachers and Students to Approach Science from a Broader Perspective." *Usable Knowledge.* Harvard Graduate School of Education, May 29, 2008. https://www.gse.harvard.edu/news/uk/08/05/connections-consequences-and-understanding.

Reviewed by Susan C. Kim, MD, Kathleen Romito, MD and John Pope, MD. "How Adolescent Thinking Develops," University of Michigan Health System, Healthwise, Inc., August 21, 2019, accessed February 2, 2021. https://www.uofmhealth.org/health-library/te7261.

Chapter 9

Centore, Anthony. "How to Forgive Yourself: Letting Go of Past Regrets," *Thriveworks* (blog), April 9, 2015. https://thriveworks.com/blog/how-to-forgive-yourself/.

Chapin, Tess. "I Lost My Virginity During a One-Night Stand, and I Regret It." *Pop Sugar,* November 28, 2019, accessed January 24, 2021. https://www.popsugar.com/love/i-lost-my-virginity-to-someone-i-didnt-care-about-46795829.

"If You Try to Please Everyone, You'll Never Find What You Are Looking For." *Exploring Your Mind* (Blog), June 15, 2018. Accessed January 25, 2021. https://exploringyourmind.com/if-you-try-to-please-everyone/.

Merriam-Webster, s.v. "Regret (n.)." Accessed October 14, 2020. https://www.merriam-webster.com/dictionary/regret.

Ruiz, Rebecca. "What It Really Means to 'Give Yourself Grace." *Mashable*, November 21, 2020. https://mashable.com/article/give-yourself-grace/.

Schulz, Kathryn. "Don't Regret Regret." Filmed November 2011 at TedStudios, New York, NY, video, 16:36. https://www.ted.com/talks/kathryn_schulz_don_t_regret_regret/transcript?language=en.

Tartakovsky, Margarita M.S. "A Powerful Exercise for Moving Past Regret." PsychCentral, September 11, 2017. https://psychcentral.com/blog/a-powerful-exercise-for-moving-past-regret#1.

Chapter 10

Bahra, Manj. "Rejection Isn't Your Reflection." *Noteworthy - The Journal Blog (blog), Medium,* June 9, 2019. Accessed January 22, 2021. https://blog.usejournal.com/rejection-isnt-your-reflection-3064f0df93bf.

Baldoni, Justin. "Why I'm Done Trying to Be 'Man Enough.'" TEDTalk, filmed November 2017 at New Orleans, LA, video, 15:22. https://www.ted.com/talks/justin_baldoni_why_i_m_done_trying_to_be_man_enough#t-178045.

Bernstein, Jeffrey, Ph.D. "Three Ways to Break Free of Your Past Relationship Baggage: Letting Go of the Past and Moving on to a Healthy Relationship." *Psychology Today. Sussex Publishers,* June 9, 2017. https://www.psychologytoday.com/us/blog/liking-the-child-you-love/201706/three-ways-break-free-your-past-relationship-baggage.

Harris, Marina, Ph.D. "You Can't Run from Your Feelings, but You can Actually Use Them to Build a Happier Life." *Medium,* September 19, 2020. Accessed January 25, 2021. https://medium.com/the-ascent/you-cant-run-from-your-feelings-4c7b651399da.

Manson, Mark. "Vulnerability: The Key to Better Relationships." Markmanson.net. Accessed January 22, 2021. https://markmanson.net/vulnerability-in-relationships.

McKibben, Shawn. "When You Begin to Accept Yourself, These 10 Amazing Things Will Happen," *Lifehack,* November 17, 2014. https://www.lifehack.org/articles/communication/

when-you-begin-accept-yourself-these-10-amazing-things-will-happen.html.

Nelson, Audrey. "Why Don't Many Men Show Their Emotions?" *Psychology Today*, Sussex Publishers, January 24, 2015. https://www.psychology-today.com/us/blog/he-speaks-she-speaks/201501/why-don-t-many-men-show-their-emotions.

Oxford English Dictionary, s.v. "Rejection (n.)." Accessed January 22, 2021. https://www.lexico.com/en/definition/rejection.

Soeiro, Loren, Ph.D. "Seven Essential Psychological Truths About Ghosting: Why 'Ghosting' Hurts So Much, Why People Do It, and How You Can Get Over It." *Psychology Today*, February 25, 2019. https://www.psychologytoday.com/us/blog/i-hear-you/201902/7-essential-psychological-truths-about-ghosting.

Van Tilburg, Kristin. "Seven Easy Ways You Can Appreciate Yourself More." *Medium*, February 4, 2019. Accessed January 22, 2021. https://medium.com/@kristinvantilburg/7-important-ways-you-can-develop-a-self-appreciation-mindset-221c6412a4d8.

Chapter 11

American Addiction Centers. "Spiked Substances." Accessed September 14, 2020. https://www.alcohol.org/guides/spiked/.

Dickinson, Kevin. "Sex, Condoms, and STDS: CDC Warns about Teen Risk Behaviors." *Big Think*,

September 2, 2020. https://bigthink.com/sex-relationships/teen-sexual-risk-behavior?rebelltitem=3#rebelltitem3.

Ketteler, Judi. "Many Teens Don't Have Sex. So Why Do Older Virgins So Often Feel Ashamed?" *Think: Opinion, Analysis, Essays*, NBC News, December 12, 2020. https://www.nbcnews.com/think/opinion/many-teens-don-t-have-sex-so-why-do-older-ncna1250928.

Live Your Dream.Org. "Domestic Violence Resources." Accessed January 21, 2021. https://www.liveyourdream.org/get-help/domestic-violence-resources.html.

Mayo Clinic. "Alcohol Poisoning." Accessed January 27, 2021. https://www.mayoclinic.org/diseases-conditions/alcohol-poisoning/symptoms-causes/syc-20354386.

Mental Health America. "Sexual Assault and Mental Health." Accessed January 27, 2021. https://www.mhanational.org/sexual-assault-and-mental-health.

Merriamebster, s.v. "Peer Pressure (n.)." Accessed October 19, 2020. https://www.merriam-webster.com/dictionary/peer%20pressure.

RAINN. "Victims of Sexual Violence: Statistics." Accessed September 14, 2020. https://www.rainn.org/statistics/victims-sexual-violence.

Vagianos, Alanna. "Thirty Alarming Statistics That Show the Reality of Sexual Violence in America: This Is What an Epidemic Looks Like." *Huffpost,* updated April 6, 2017.

https://www.huffpost.com/entry/sexual-assault-statisti
cs_n_58e24c14e4b0c777f788d24f?guccounter=1&guce_
referrer=aHR0cHM6Ly93d3cuZ29vZ2xlLmNvbS88&guce_
referrer_sig=AQAAAGqwiDvtd4HuBiO7UgxA_mH5WA7O-
XT9MIw7XQjq3N0HRocjwxjHsGuEUqz8JvsTm_3CfQlRm
gym-5xRnyHRq6DV9HlJLsRFuHD9xrfUwznyQCe2x6AQ
AJViuswH7EY_3YMo9aCF-AQG6gcpt3OzjASjv9flhCeYdN
V_2loot6ko.

Chapter 12

DiGregorio, Jaclyn. *The Cusp Method: Your Guide to Balanced Portions and a Healthy Life*. New Degree Press, 2017.

DiGregorio, Jaclyn. *Stop Getting in Your Own Way: A No B.S. Guide to Creating the Business of Your Dreams*. New Degree Press, 2019.

Holohan, Meghan. "Reach Out to an Old Friend—Research Says It Is a Mood Booster." *Mind & Body, Today*, April 30, 2020. https://www.today.com/health/reconnecting-old-friends-helps-during-coronavirus-crisis-t180416.

Hudson, Paul. "Be Spontaneous: The 6 Reasons You Should Never Make a Plan Again." *Elite Daily*, January 21, 2014. https://www.elitedaily.com/life/motivation/six-reasons-making-plans-may-bad-idea.

James, Alfred. "How to Adapt to Change When You Want to Resist." *Pocket Mindfulness* (blog). Accessed October 26, 2020. https://www.pocketmindfulness.com/adapt-to-change/.

Lurie, Saba Harouni. "The Power of Reaching Out: Showing Up for Others." Take Root Therapy, June 14, 2018. Accessed October 25, 2020. https://www.losangelesmftherapist.com/post/the-power-of-reaching-out-showing-up-for-others.

McFarland, Colleen. *Disconnected: How to Use People Data to Deliver Realness, Meaning, and Belonging at Work.* New Degree Press, 2020.

Oxford Learner's Dictionary, s.v. "Adaptability (*n.*)." Accessed February 8, 2021. https://www.oxfordlearnersdictionaries.com/us/definition/english/adaptability?q=adaptability.

Sanford, Kathryn. "Adapting to Change: Why It Matters and How to Do It." *Success Mindset,* Lifehack, January 12, 2021. Accessed January 25, 2021. https://www.lifehack.org/372463/why-you-need-adapt-change.

Chapter 13

Altshul, Sara. "Fourteen Celebrities Who Have Experienced Depression." *Everyday Health,* March 4, 2016. Accessed September 13, 2020. https://www.everydayhealth.com/pictures/celebrities-who-have-experienced-depression/.

Becker, Joshua. "Nine Reasons Buying Stuff Will Never Make You Happy." *Becoming Minimalist* (blog). Accessed October 30, 2020. https://www.becomingminimalist.com/buying-stuff-wont-make-you-happy/.

Bryner, Jeanna. "Realities of One-Night Stands Revealed." *Live Science,* July 10, 2008. https://www.livescience.com/2678-realities-night-stands-revealed.html.

Merriam-Webster, s.v. "Unbreakable (adj.)." Accessed October 29, 2020. https://www.merriam-webster.com/dictionary/unbreakable.

Rutledge, Pamela B., Ph.D. "The Psychological Power of Storytelling: Stories Leap-Frog Technology, Taking Us to Authentic Experience." *Psychology Today,* January 16, 2011. https://www.psychologytoday.com/us/blog/positively-media/201101/the-psychological-power-storytelling.

Samaha, Barry. "The Best Coco Chanel Quotes about Fashion, Love, and Success." Harper's Bazaar, June 25, 2020. https://www.harpersbazaar.com/fashion/designers/g32971271/best-coco-chanel-quotes/#:~:text=1%20%22Elegance%20is%20refusal.%22&text=2%20%22In%20order%20to%20be,one%20must%20always%20be%20different.%22.

Thomas, Madison. *Redefining: What 32 Surgeries Taught Me about How to View Life and My Body.* Self-published, 2020. *https://www.madisonthomas.org/redefining.*

Thompson, Brian. "When Enough is Enough: Confronting the Ego." *Zen Thinking* (blog), November 19, 2015. Accessed October 30, 2020. http://www.zenthinking.net/blog/when-enough-is-enough-confronting-the-ego.

Acknowledgments

———

Thank you to my incredible friends, I couldn't have done this without you.

Thank you to my parents as well for believing in my me and trusting that I can do anything if I put my mind to it. You both are the most incredible people I know. I love you and thank you for all you have given me. I am so blessed to have you guys as parents.

Sana Mitra and family thank you from the bottom of my heart for everything you have done. I couldn't have gotten here without you guys. Thank you, love you guys.

Julia Ruggiero thank you for making me believe I could do this and publish a book. You are the one that helped me start all of it so thank you. You believed I could do it. You are such an incredible friend. Love you.

Sara Miller thank you for believing in me throughout this whole process. Thank you for your positive energy and your friendship through this journey. Thank you for your love and support, I love you a lot.

Maddie Lucey thanks for pushing me out of my comfort zone and making me believe I could accomplish this. You're an amazing friend and I appreciate you. Love you always.

Jordan Payson we have been friends for years and I am so grateful we met each other. We have believed in each other and supported each other since the beginning. You believed I could do this and I thank you for your love and support. You are such an incredible person. I love you.

Rebecca Grady thanks for being so supportive and always there for me. I could not have made it through this without you. You have such a special place in my heart. I appreciate you and our friendship beyond words. I am so happy boarding school brought us together.

Vanessa Block thanks for being so strong and being able to help me really share what is on my heart. You have helped me become stronger and together our friendship has grown too. I love you and am thankful for our friendship.

Thank you to everyone at New Degree Press who helped my book come to life. Thank you to my amazing editors who helped me along the way.

Thank you to Eric Koester, Brian Pies, Paige Buxbaum, Linda Berdelli, Annabelle Libanan, Kayla LeFevre, Leila Summers, Julie Colvin, Gjorji Pejkovski and Melody Delgado Lorbeer.

Thank you to all of my amazing friends and family for their continued love and support.

Jordan Skowron I know I mentioned you earlier but you really have helped me grow into the person I am today. Thank you, I love you.

Jackson Landman although we might not have the most conventual kind of relationship, thank you for being there and cheering me on always. You are such a special friend and always will be. Love you Jacks.

Ali Bello- You deserve the world. You are forever my fighter. Thanks for helping me keep a positive mindset throughout this process. You are my inspiration, and I am so proud of you. You make every situation positive. Keep fighting Al because there is a light at the end of the tunnel. I love you my smushy.

And last but certainly not least Naomi Grossman. You are my forever angel and I am so grateful to have you in my life. Thank you for being there always. I love you so much and could not thank you enough for all that you have done for me. I love you forever my best friend.

Thank you as well to the people who supported my presale campaign. This book would not have been possible without:

- Naomi Grossman
- Jackson Landman
- Naomi Rossman
- Jennifer DeSancis
- Katie Rozier
- Lindsey Bost
- Jaclyn DiGregorio
- Justin Hardin
- Alexa Smith
- Meghan Amayo
- Fay Blelloch
- Benjamin Griffths
- Robynne Smith
- Nicole Giannangeli

- Ronna Riffle
- Carin Harkness
- Anna Salzman
- Lexy Hollis
- John Skowron
- Aditya Desai
- Julia Ruggiero
- Vanessa Steiner
- Jordan Skowron
- Connie Lucey
- Jacob Gerszten
- Emily Carlson
- Paige Buxbaum
- Eric Koester
- Geena Provenzano
- Elizabeth Knappenberger
- Shellie Wharton
- Emmelia Jaffe
- Charlie Nectow
- Krisanne Shideler
- Lucy King
- Michele Donahoe
- Elyse Kraft
- Shannon Sinwell
- Stephanie Newrones
- Sandra Skowron
- Catherine Bannister
- Meredith Jayme
- Peggy Jayme
- Deborah DeLong
- John Gibbons
- Abdesalam Soudi
- Vikram Kapoor
- Caroline Rice
- Cristal Casellas
- Christine Luketich
- Robert Cunliffe
- Anika Dholakia
- Anne Reid
- Elizabeth Manuck
- Gabrielle Lisella
- Taylor Yester
- Sarah Kintner
- Hannah Kalchthaler
- Michelle King
- Nancy Harvey
- Allison Herdje
- Heather Cullinan
- Maggie McIlroy
- Maddie Lucey
- Colleen McFarland
- John Cunliffe
- Susan Skowron

39020646R00116